Empowering Your Under 10

Essential Life Skills Handbook

Oaklyn Reid

OAKLYN
PUBLISHING

Copyright © 2023 by Oaklyn Reid

All rights reserved.

The contents of this book may not be reproduced, duplicated, or transmitted without direct written permission from the author.

For Michael, Lucy and Emma

Contents

Introduction 1

Section 1: Age 2-3 Years Old 3

1. Becoming Independent 5
   Basic Self-Care Skills
   Encouraging Independence In Simple Tasks
   Building Confidence Through Small Responsibilities

2. Nurturing a Clean Environment 15
   Introduction To Basic Cleaning Up
   Promoting The Value Of Cleanliness And Organization

3. Staying Safe 23
   Learning To Be Safe In Different Surroundings
   Buckle Up Challenge
   Helmet On!
   Not running off
   Introduce Emergency Numbers
   Learn How To Dial A Number

4. Feelings and Emotions at a Young Age 35

　　　　Effective Communication skills
　　　　Talk About Needs to Encourage Expression and Thinking
　　　　Managing emotions
　　　　Learning Good Manners
　　　　Interacting with other children

5. Learning Early Motor Skills　　　　　　　　　　　　47
　　　　Fine Motor Skills:
　　　　Gross Motor Skills:
　　　　Running:
　　　　Jumping:
　　　　Climbing:
　　　　Catching:

Section 2: Age 4-6 Years Old　　　　　　　　　　　　54

6. Developing Life Skills In Everyday Tasks　　　　　55
　　　　Self-Care
　　　　Dressing And Undressing
　　　　The Virtue Of "Cleaning"
　　　　Basic Cleaning Skills
　　　　Basic Kitchen Skills
　　　　Learning Basic Technology
　　　　Value And Taking Care Of Belongings

7. Safety and Emergency Preparedness　　　　　　　73
　　　　Introduction To Emergency Services:
　　　　Promoting Safety Habits
　　　　Stranger Danger

8. Learning More Advanced Motor Skills　　　　　　81
　　　　How To Ride A Bike?
　　　　Learning To Swim
　　　　Introduce Letters and Numbers:

9. Caring for Living Things — 91
   Caring For Plants
   Caring For A Pet
   Visit Farms And Zoos
   Waste Management for a Healthier Environment

10. Feelings and Emotions when Interacting With Others — 101
    Overcoming Shyness
    Making Friends
    Enhancing Communication Skills

Section 3: Age 6-10 Years Old — 109

11. Improve Reading and Communication Skills — 111
    Learn To Love Reading
    How To Communicate and Write Effectively

12. Practical Skills — 121
    Household Tasks
    DIY Jobs:

13. Managing Emotions and Problem-Solving — 133
    Recognizing And Expressing Emotions
    Strategies For Problem-Solving and Decision-Making
    Building Resilience and Coping Skills

14. Facing Fears and Building Confidence — 147
    Addressing Common Fears and Anxieties
    Encouraging Bravery and Trying New Things
    Developing Self-Confidence and Self-Esteem

15. Navigating Social Skills and Relationships — 157
    Understanding The Importance of Kindness and Empathy
    Developing Effective Communication Skills
    Resolving Conflicts and Making Friends

Conclusion 169

References 171

Introduction

Prepare the child for the path, not the path for the child." - Native American proverb.

Welcome to "Empowering your Under 10: Essential Life Skills Handbook," where we embark on a transformative journey together. This book is dedicated to empowering our young ones with invaluable skills that will enable them to navigate life's challenges with confidence and grace. Far beyond just another parenting manual, it serves as an expedition into uncharted territories of nurturing growing minds and hearts.

Children possess an innate ability to absorb information effortlessly, but what they soak up profoundly shapes their personalities and future paths. By reading this book, you show a dedication to guiding your child toward absorbing the right things—essential values, life skills, and lessons that will lead them to triumph in life.

Within these pages, we'll discover how to inspire independence in children as young as two or three and uncover the secrets to fostering a clean environment and promoting safety awareness. We'll also delve into the realm of emotions, while simultaneously introducing motor skills learning.

As we progress further into this adventure, we'll explore chapters dedicated to children aged between four and five years old. The focus here lies in developing life skills through seemingly mundane everyday tasks that hold profound lessons within themselves. Remember Arthur Conan Doyle's wisdom: 'The little things are infinitely the most important'? Indeed, he was on to something.

But we won't stop there. For our older group of six-to-ten-year-olds, we'll delve into essential practical skills such as cultivating a love for reading, employing effective writing techniques (no boring grammar drills involved!), managing emotions effectively (yes, even at tender ages), facing fears head-on with a superhero's courage, building unshakable confidence, and mastering the art of navigating social relationships with ease.

So fasten your seatbelts because this journey may get bumpy! But remember, every bump is a lesson waiting to be learned, and every turn presents an opportunity to be seized. As a fellow parent who has traveled these winding roads before, I promise you're not alone.

So let's uncover the well-kept secrets of childhood development in its most natural form—learning by doing—and open doors of opportunity for your little ones. Making things easy for your kids doesn't help them in the long run, and after all, isn't empowering a child-like equipping them with wings strong enough to soar high yet gentle enough to touch lives? Together, let's nurture resilient children who are prepared for whatever lies ahead.

Section 1: Age 2-3 Years Old

BECOMING INDEPENDENT

Now, you might be wondering, "Why should I encourage independence in my toddler at such a young age?" Let's shed some light on the matter. Picture this: Have you ever tried to put shoes on a wriggling octopus with a mind of its own? Or attempted to feed an enthusiastic toddler who insists on wielding the spoon like a magic wand? Embracing independence in your little ones can actually lead to some delightful moments. Just envision the joy of witnessing your two-year-old attempting to put on their own pants, resulting in both legs somehow finding their way into one hole. It's like a comical game of toddler Twister that leaves everyone in fits of laughter!

Encouraging independence also means embracing chaos. Get ready for the infamous "I do it myself" phase, where your little one insists on dressing themselves but ends up wearing mismatched socks, inside-out pants, and a superhero cape as a hat. Fashion icons in the making, we say! Remember, laughter is the secret ingredient to surviving parenthood, and teaching independence is the key to raising confident, resourceful, and utterly entertaining little humans.

It's incredible to witness how determined toddlers can be when they want to do things on their own! Encouraging their independence is not only adorable but also vital for their growth. Allowing them to make choices, tackle simple tasks, and explore their own capabilities helps foster a sense of autonomy and self-reliance. Of course, it's essential to strike a balance between letting them spread their wings and providing guidance when needed.

Basic Self-Care Skills

Introducing basic self-care skills to your adorable 2-3-year-old tornadoes is like setting off on a wild and exhilarating adventure. Buckle up because you're about to enter a world of sudsy chaos and toothpaste splatters that will leave you both giggling and slightly exasperated. But fear not because, in the midst of the mess, you'll witness your little ones blossoming into independent beings with a newfound sense of accomplishment.

Start With Face-Washing

To make face-washing a fun and interactive activity for children, you can start by choosing a child-friendly, tear-free soap that is gentle on their skin. When introducing the activity, first take a moment to explain to your little one the purpose behind it. Let them know that by washing their face, they are removing all the dirt and impurities, leaving their skin fresh and clean. This simple explanation can help them understand the importance of maintaining good hygiene while making the activity more engaging. Since children love to copy their parents, if you keep them around to see you washing your own face, they will try to do the same. And when they do that, make sure to offer your help and guidance through this.

You can enhance the experience by making it a game for them. You can give a soft cloth or sponge to your kids and demonstrate the proper face-washing technique, encouraging them to imitate your moves. This element of imitation can make the activity more enjoyable and help your child feel involved. However, it's essential to be prepared for some water splashing and perhaps some "artistic" face painting, as children may get creative during the process. Embrace their enthusiasm and make sure to have a towel nearby to clean up any messes and keep the activity enjoyable for everyone involved.

Brushing Teeth

This will not only help improve the dental hygiene of your toddler, but it will also make him habitual to brush his teeth every night. To make this activity engaging, start by selecting a colorful child-sized toothbrush. Introduce the toothbrush as their superhero sidekick, explaining that it will help them fight off the sneaky sugar bugs that can harm their teeth. By personifying the toothbrush in this way, you can create a playful and imaginative connection that can make brushing more exciting for your toddler.

To make teeth brushing even more enjoyable, incorporate music into the routine. Sing silly songs or play your child's favorite tunes while they brush their teeth. Music adds an element of fun and rhythm to the activity, making it feel like a memorable and enjoyable moment in their daily routine. Additionally, encourage your child to show off their "pearly whites" by making funny toothy smiles in the mirror. This lighthearted and amusing gesture can bring laughter and create positive associations with oral hygiene.

Wash Hands

Begin by explaining the importance of handwashing in keeping them healthy and strong. Emphasize that by washing their hands, they can help prevent the spread of germs and stay well. Instead of giving them a long lecture on the subject, use visual aids like storybooks and images of their favorite cartoon characters washing hands to influence their young minds. To make the process more accessible, consider using a step stool or a child-sized sink that allows them to reach comfortably and engage in the activity independently.

Demonstrate the proper handwashing technique to your child by simply doing it in front of them. You will be amazed by how quickly they will pick it up. Show them how to wet their hands thoroughly, apply soap, and scrub all the nooks and crannies of their hands for at least 20 seconds. To make the process more enjoyable and engaging, incorporate a catchy tune like the ABC song or any other song they find fun. Singing a song while they wash helps them keep track of the recommended time duration for effective handwashing. It may mean singing "Happy Birthday" or other tunes multiple times a day, but the benefits of instilling this healthy habit in your child far outweigh the repetition.

Encouraging Independence In Simple Tasks

Encouraging independence in young children can be an exhilarating journey for parents. And this process literally starts with baby steps. You can start with the simplest of tasks, like teaching them to pick up their own toys and put them back in their place. Doing such simple tasks, your child will feel empowered, and it will instill a sense of accomplishment in them, which is a must when it comes to building confidence and making them independent. While it may bring a certain level of chaos, it also presents an opportunity for growth and development. By empowering your children to take on tasks like picking up toys, choosing clothes, and dressing themselves, you are nurturing their sense of autonomy and self-reliance.

Picking Up Toys

To encourage your child to pick up toys and maintain a tidy play area, it's essential to establish a designated toy storage area. This can be achieved through the use of colorful bins, shelves, or a toy chest. Teach your child that each toy has its own particular home and demonstrate how to place toys back in their designated spots properly. By providing a clear structure and routine, you can help them develop the habit of tidying up after playtime.

Transforming the task of tidying up into a fun activity can make it more engaging for your child. You can turn it into a game, set a timer to create a sense of urgency and excitement or play some upbeat music to make the process enjoyable. This not only adds an element of fun but also creates a positive association with cleaning up. While it's inevitable that you may still find toys in unexpected places like the fridge or inside your shoes, remember that their efforts should be celebrated. Try to encourage your child's attempts and provide gentle guidance to help them improve their tidying skills over time.

By creating a designated toy storage area and making tidying up a fun activity, you can instill good organizational habits in your child. This not only helps keep their play area neat and tidy but also teaches them valuable life skills such as responsibility and self-discipline. Remember to be patient and supportive as they learn, acknowledging their efforts and progress along the way.

Choosing Clothes

As your child exercises their independence, be prepared for some exciting clothing combinations that may not conform to traditional fashion norms. It's important to embrace their unique sense of style and allow them to express their creativity. Letting them wear mismatched socks or layer a superhero cape over a princess dress can be a way for them to assert their individuality and explore their imagination. Encouraging their self-expression in clothing choices helps build their confidence and allows them to develop a sense of personal identity. Remember, there are no strict rules when it comes to fashion, and embracing their creativity can lead to delightful surprises and cherished memories.

Encouraging independence in choosing clothes for your child can be a great way to foster their sense of individuality and self-expression. Start by curating a wardrobe that offers a variety of weather-appropriate and occasion-specific options. Lay out a few choices for your child to select from, allowing them to make their own decisions. This gives them a sense of autonomy and helps them develop their personal style preferences.

Dressing Oneself

Teaching your child to dress themselves is a significant milestone in their journey toward independence. When selecting clothes for them, opt for garments with simple closures such as elastic waistbands or large buttons. These types of clothing make it easier for your child to manipulate and put on by themselves.

To help them learn the process of dressing, demonstrate step-by-step how to put on clothes. It's good to encourage them to do it themselves, providing gentle guidance and support as needed. It's essential to be patient during this learning phase, as there may be moments when they struggle or make mistakes like putting shirts on backward or pants inside-out. These are all part of the learning process, and it's crucial to celebrate their efforts and progress along the way.

While it may be tempting to step in and dress your child quickly to save time, it's essential to resist that urge and allow them to take on the task themselves. Even if it takes a bit longer, allowing them the space to learn and practice promotes their independence and builds their self-confidence.

Building Confidence Through Small Responsibilities

Building confidence in our little ones is like watching a tiny seed blossom into a beautiful flower. And one way to nurture their self-assurance is by giving them small responsibilities. Since, at this stage, the children are too young to take their own big responsibility, you can start with a few of the most basic ones, like potty training and putting away their dirty clothes.

Potty Training

Introducing your child to the concept of using the potty is a significant step towards independence and building their confidence. To make this transition exciting, approach it with a positive attitude. Decorate the potty with colorful stickers or allow them to choose a special potty seat that they find appealing. By personalizing the potty, you create a sense of ownership and make it a more engaging experience for your child.

To further make potty training fun and enjoyable, incorporate playful elements into the process. Sing silly songs or read funny books about using the potty to create a lighthearted atmosphere. Encourage your child to sit on the potty regularly, even if they don't actually go. This helps them become familiar with the routine and encourages them to establish a habit. Celebrate their small successes with praise, high-fives, and even a potty dance, turning the accomplishment into a joyful and rewarding experience. Utilizing a sticker chart to track their progress can also be a visual representation of their achievements, motivating them to continue their potty training journey.

By approaching potty training with positivity, excitement, and fun, you empower your child to take ownership of this developmental milestone. Creating an engaging environment with decorations, incorporating songs and books, and celebrating their progress builds their confidence and instills a sense of accomplishment. With time and consistent support, your little one will proudly declare mastery over the potty, marking a significant step towards independence.

Dirty Clothes into Hamper

Teaching your children to put their dirty clothes into the hamper not only helps keep their living space tidy but also fosters a sense of confidence and responsibility. To start, make sure there is a child-friendly hamper within their reach, making it easy for them to access and use. Demonstrate how to toss clothes into the hamper and turn it into a playful game. Pretend the hamper is a basketball hoop, encouraging them to score points every time they successfully make a shot. This playful approach adds an element of fun and turns a chore into an exciting activity.

Throughout the process, provide plenty of praise and encouragement for their efforts. Celebrate each successful toss, regardless of the occasional stray sock that may end up in unexpected places like the ceiling fan. Remember that these moments are part of the adventure of learning and growing. By offering positive reinforcement, you nurture their sense of accomplishment and motivation to continue practicing this responsibility. With time, your little laundry hero will proudly declare their commitment to keeping the environment clean, exclaiming, "No dirty clothes shall escape my sight!"

By involving your children in the process of putting dirty clothes in the hamper, you empower them with a sense of responsibility and independence. Transforming this task into a game and providing praise for their efforts turns it into an enjoyable and engaging experience. As they learn to take charge of their dirty laundry, they develop essential life skills and a sense of pride in contributing to a tidy living space. Embrace the adventure and celebrate their progress along the way!

Nurturing a Clean Environment

Introducing the concept of cleaning the environment to 2-3-year-olds is incredibly important, and parents play a vital role in teaching them about it from an early age. You might be wondering why it is so crucial to teach little ones about cleaning. Well, let me break it down for you. Teaching toddlers about cleaning instills in them a sense of responsibility and ownership. By involving them in tidying up their surroundings, we empower them to take pride in their environment. They begin to understand that they have a role to play in keeping their living spaces clean and organized.

Introducing cleaning at a young age helps children develop essential life skills. They learn about hygiene, organization, and the value of cleanliness. These skills will serve them well as they grow older and navigate various environments, whether it's their home, school, or public spaces. As they learn how to pick up their toys, wipe a spill, or help with simple household tasks, they gain confidence in their abilities. They begin to understand that they are capable of contributing to the upkeep of their surroundings, no matter how small the task.

When children learn the importance of cleanliness from the start, it becomes a natural part of their routine. It becomes second nature for them to tidy up after themselves, respect their surroundings, and appreciate the value of a clean environment.

Introduction To Basic Cleaning Up

The quest for a clean and tidy home with young children is like trying to catch a rainbow with a butterfly net! Maintaining a clean and tidy home with young children can sometimes feel like an elusive goal. However, there are strategies that can transform this challenge into an enjoyable adventure for both parents and children alike. The key is to strike a balance between cleanliness and playfulness, allowing your little ones to participate in the process while fostering their sense of responsibility. One approach is to turn cleaning into a game or a fun activity. For example, you can create a "treasure hunt" where your child helps you find and put away items in their designated places. Use colorful bins or labels to make it visually appealing and engaging for them. Another idea is to set a timer and turn cleaning into a race, challenging your child to complete tasks within a specific timeframe. This can make cleaning feel exciting and motivate them to participate actively.

Putting Away Toys

To make the task of tidying up toys more exciting, infuse it with creativity and imagination. Create a catchy cleanup song that your children can sing along to as they pick up their toys. Alternatively, invent a magical story where the toys come to life and need to find their designated spots in their toy kingdom. This storytelling element adds an element of adventure and engages your little helpers in a fun way.

Empower your children by assigning them specific toy categories to organize, such as "superheroes" or "dolls." This gives them a sense of responsibility and ownership over the cleanup process. You can also introduce a time element to make it more thrilling. Challenge them to beat their previous cleanup record or turn it into a race against the clock. By setting goals and creating a sense of friendly competition, your living room will soon transform into a toy-free paradise.

As your children take charge of tidying up and successfully completing the task, their sense of accomplishment will be evident. They will beam with pride, declaring themselves the champions of cleanliness. This positive reinforcement and recognition for their efforts further encourage them to actively participate in keeping their living space tidy. By infusing the cleanup process with excitement and playfulness, you create an enjoyable environment where your little ones learn the importance of cleanliness while having fun along the way.

Clean Up the Spills

When spills occur, it's a perfect opportunity to engage your little ones in the cleanup process and turn it into a fun and empowering experience. Equip them with their own mini-sized cleaning supplies, such as a small cloth or paper towel and a spray bottle filled with water (avoiding the use of chemicals). By giving them their own tools, you create a sense of responsibility and ownership over the task.

Teach them how to gently wipe spills, turning them into a playful game of "Magical Cleanup Wizards." Encourage their imagination by framing the task as banishing evil stains and saving the day. Praise their efforts and cheer them on as they work their magic, one spill at a time. It's essential to be prepared for some giggles, the occasional missed spot, and the triumphant cry of "We have vanquished the spills, Mom and Dad!" This positive reinforcement and celebration of their accomplishment reinforces their sense of empowerment and nurtures their willingness to help out in keeping the environment clean.

Plates to the Sink

After a satisfying meal, it's time to cultivate responsible mealtime champions in your little ones. Empower them to take their plates to the sink, transforming this task into an enjoyable and engaging activity. Turn it into a fun relay race, where they pass the plates to each other, creating a sense of teamwork and camaraderie. Or by adding an element of excitement to the task, they could scrape any dog friendly scraps into Buster's bowl for a treat, or even into the compost if that is the setup at home. Help them to understand why we do things a certain way so that they can digest the information and remember for next time.

When they successfully complete their task, celebrate their achievement with applause and a silly victory dance. This acknowledgment of their efforts and accomplishment reinforces their sense of responsibility and encourages them to participate in household tasks actively. By infusing mealtime cleanup with excitement and celebration, you create a positive atmosphere where your little ones take pride in their responsible actions.

Exploring Simple Chores

Encouraging children to explore simple chores can be a great way to introduce them to responsibility and develop their skills. Show your children how to do the chores by demonstrating the proper techniques yourself. Explain the purpose and importance of each chore in a way that they can understand. For example, you can explain that dusting helps to keep surfaces clean and free from allergens. Choose chores that are suitable for your child's age and abilities. For young children, start with simple tasks that they can quickly grasp and perform, such as dusting low surfaces or sweeping small areas. As they grow older and more capable, you can gradually introduce more complex chores.

Provide Child-Sized Tools: Invest in child-sized cleaning tools like a mini broom, a dusting cloth, or a small handheld duster. Having tools that are specifically designed for their size will make the chores more manageable and enjoyable for them. It also gives them a sense of ownership and independence.

Create a Cleaning Kit: Assemble a cleaning kit with all the necessary supplies for your child's chores. This can include their mini broom, dusting cloth, spray bottle with a mild cleaning solution (if applicable), and a small dustpan. Having their own kit will make them feel special and prepared for their cleaning tasks.

Break it Down: Break the chore into smaller steps and guide your child through each one. For example, when dusting, you can start by showing them how to hold the cloth properly, how to wipe surfaces gently, and how to reach different areas. As they become more proficient, allow them to complete the steps independently.

Turn it into a Game: Make chores fun by turning them into a game or a challenge. You can set a timer and see how quickly your child can sweep a particular area or turn dusting into a treasure hunt, where they have to find and clean hidden objects. Adding an element of fun and competition can make the chores more exciting for your child.

Offer Guidance and Support: Be present to offer guidance and support as your child explores chores. Provide encouragement, praise their efforts, and offer gentle corrections when needed. Let them know that their contribution is valued and appreciated.

Gradually Increase Responsibility: As your child becomes more comfortable with the initial chores, gradually increase their responsibilities. Introduce new tasks or expand the areas they are responsible for cleaning. This helps them develop a sense of competence and builds their confidence in taking on more challenging chores.

Promoting The Value Of Cleanliness And Organization

Children learn by observing and imitating their parents. Show them the importance of cleanliness and organization by practicing it yourself. Let them see you tidying up, cleaning, and organizing your own spaces. They will naturally pick up on your habits and understand that it's a valuable aspect of daily life.

Turn cleaning and organizing into a game to engage your children's imagination and make it enjoyable. For example, you can have a "Race Against the Mess" where they try to clean up their toys before a timer goes off. Use playful language and give them exciting missions like being "Super Cleanup Heroes" or "Mess Detectives" to make the tasks more exciting. Establish a daily routine that includes specific times for cleaning and organizing. Make it a regular part of their day, just like eating or playing. Having a predictable schedule will help them understand that cleanliness and organization are essential components of their daily lives.

Young children can easily get overwhelmed with extensive cleaning or organizing tasks. Break them down into smaller, manageable steps. For example, instead of telling them to clean their entire room, you can ask them to start by picking up their toys and then later move on to organizing their books or clothes. Celebrate each completed step to keep them motivated. Give your children age-appropriate cleaning tools such as a small broom, dustpan, or a mini cleaning kit. Having their own tools will make them feel important and encourage their participation in cleaning tasks. You can also let them choose fun and colorful storage bins or boxes to keep their belongings organized.

Recognize and appreciate your children's efforts in maintaining cleanliness and organization. Offer specific praise when they complete a task or make progress, highlighting their accomplishments. This positive reinforcement will motivate them to continue their efforts. When organizing spaces or deciding where things should go, involve your children in the decision-making process. Ask for their opinions and let them contribute their ideas. This will give them a sense of ownership and responsibility for their environment.

Staying Safe

Toddlers have a way of finding themselves in the most unexpected situations. One minute, they're happily exploring the world, and the next, they're attempting daredevil stunts worthy of an action movie. That's why it's crucial to teach them about safety from an early age in a way that's both educational and mildly humorous. Picture this: your little one decides they're a superhero and wants to fly off the couch. As much as we'd love to see them soar through the air, it's our duty to explain that humans aren't equipped with wings. Using a touch of humor, we can remind them that even superheroes need to be sensibly safe too. "You know, my little superhero, flying is best left to the professionals. How about we find a safer way to enjoy our adventures?"

And who can forget the classic game of "'The Floor Is Lava"? It's a rite of passage for every toddler. Amidst the imaginary hot lava and leaps of faith, we can weave in essential safety lessons. With a twinkle in our eye, we can say, "Oh no, the floor has turned into lava! Quick, find a safe spot like a pillow island or a fluffy cloud. We don't want our little explorer getting burned!"

Teaching safety to our 2-3-year-olds isn't just about protecting them from potential hazards; it's about nurturing their growing independence. By introducing safety concepts early on, we give them the tools to navigate their surroundings with confidence. Plus, let's be honest; it's a great way to keep our hearts from leaping out of our chests every time they venture into the unknown.

Learning To Be Safe In Different Surroundings

Teaching young children to be safe in different surroundings is essential for their well-being. Begin by introducing basic safety concepts in a way that is age-appropriate and easy for your child to understand. For example, explain that wearing a seatbelt keeps them safe in the car or wearing a helmet protects their head while riding a bike or scooter.

Children often learn by imitating their parents or caregivers. Show them the importance of following safety rules by consistently modeling safe behaviors yourself. Demonstrate wearing a seatbelt when you're in the car together or wearing a helmet when you ride a bike. Utilize visual aids, such as pictures, diagrams, or books, to reinforce safety rules and concepts. Show them pictures of children wearing seatbelts or helmets, and explain why it is essential. Visuals can help them grasp the concept and remember to follow safety guidelines.

Regularly practice safety routines and rules with your child. For example, practice putting on and adjusting a seatbelt or helmet together, emphasizing that it is a necessary step before starting any activity. Repetition helps reinforce the habit and makes it more likely for your child to remember and follow safety procedures. Use simple language to explain the potential consequences of not following safety guidelines. For instance, explain that not wearing a seatbelt could result in injury during a sudden stop or collision or not wearing a helmet could lead to a head injury. Make sure to emphasize that following safety rules helps keep them safe and healthy.

Establish clear and age-appropriate safety rules for different environments, such as the home, car, park, or playground. Make these rules simple and easy to understand, and consistently reinforce them. For example, "Hold an adult's hand when crossing the street" or "Always wear a helmet when riding a bike." Praise and reward your child when they demonstrate safe behavior. Positive reinforcement can motivate them to continue following safety guidelines. Celebrate their efforts and highlight how their actions contribute to their well-being.

Teach your child to communicate their concerns or ask for help when they feel unsafe. Encourage open dialogue and let them know they can approach you or a trusted adult if they encounter a situation that makes them uncomfortable or unsure. Teach your child to be aware of their surroundings and potential hazards. For example, teach them to look both ways before crossing the street, be cautious around unfamiliar dogs, or avoid touching hot surfaces. Teach them to use their senses (sight, hearing, touch) to assess their environment.

Incorporate safety lessons into playtime and exploration. Set up scenarios where they can practice safety skills, such as "driving" toy cars and buckling up their dolls or teddy bears with mini seatbelts. This playful approach helps reinforce safety rules in a fun and engaging manner.

Buckle Up Challenge

Time to buckle up into a game by creating a "buckle-up challenge." Use a toy car or pretend you're going on an exciting adventure together. Encourage your child to buckle their toy or themselves into their car seat or booster seat, just like you buckle up in the car. Celebrate their success with praise and a high-five! Make it a routine and emphasize that everyone in the family wears seat belts to stay safe.

Create visual reminders in the car to reinforce the habit of wearing seat belts. Draw or print pictures of seat belts and display them near your child's car seat. You can also find age-appropriate books or videos that explain seat belt safety and watch them together. Encourage your child's imagination by having conversations about car journeys and the exciting things they'll see along the way. Talk about the adventures you'll have and the places you'll visit, emphasizing that wearing a seat belt is an integral part of the journey.

Keep your explanations simple and age-appropriate. Explain that seat belts keep them safe by holding them securely in their seat, just like a big hug from a friend. Emphasize that it's essential to wear a seat belt every time they get in the car, no matter how short the journey.

Helmet On!

Find a children's book or create a simple story that emphasizes the importance of wearing a helmet. Use colorful illustrations and relatable characters to capture your child's attention. Make the story interactive by asking questions and involving your child in the storytelling process. Get a child-sized helmet that fits your little one comfortably. Let your child explore and play with the helmet, allowing them to become familiar with it. Encourage them to touch and try it on, making it a positive and exciting experience.

Engage in imaginative play by pretending to go on a bike ride or scooter adventure. Dress up your child in their helmet and let them "ride" around the house or yard. Reinforce the idea that wearing a helmet is an essential part of any exciting adventure. Look for pictures or videos of children wearing helmets while biking, skating, or participating in other activities. Point out how the helmet protects their heads and keeps them safe. Make it a game to spot characters or people wearing helmets in books, movies, or when you're out and about.

Lead by example and wear your own helmet when you engage in activities where head protection is necessary. Explain to your child why you wear a helmet and how it keeps you safe. Let them see that helmet-wearing is a family habit. Whenever you and your child engage in activities that require a helmet, make it a routine to wear it every time. Consistency helps establish the habit and reinforces the importance of wearing a helmet for safety. Celebrate and acknowledge your child's efforts and willingness to wear a helmet. Use words of encouragement and offer small rewards, such as stickers or a special treat, to reinforce positive behavior.

Not running off

Establish clear boundaries and communicate them to your child. Use simple and consistent language to explain where it is safe for them to play and explore. For example, you can say, "We stay together in the park, and we don't run away." Use visual aids such as signs or colorful tape to mark boundaries. This can help your child visually understand where they are allowed to go and why they should not venture off. When in busy or crowded places, hold your child's hand firmly to keep them close. Alternatively, you can use a safety harness or a child leash to provide them with a sense of independence while ensuring their safety. Teach your child simple commands like "Stop" and "Come" to help them understand when they need to pause or return to you. Practice these commands in a safe and controlled environment, such as your backyard or a quiet area of the park.

Engage your child in games that encourage them to stay near you. For example, you can play "Follow the Leader," where they need to mimic your movements while staying by your side. This game helps them understand the concept of staying close and following your lead. When your child stays close and follows your instructions, provide them with praise and positive reinforcement. Celebrate their efforts and let them know that you appreciate their cooperation. This will encourage them to continue behaving appropriately. Tell stories or create scenarios where characters learn the importance of staying close to their caregivers. Use toys or stuffed animals to act out these situations, allowing your child to understand the consequences of running off.

Introduce Emergency Numbers

Start by teaching your child the emergency numbers, such as 911 or the local emergency hotline in your country. Repeat the numbers regularly, emphasizing their importance and purpose. Make it a fun and engaging activity by incorporating songs, rhymes, or visual aids to help them remember the numbers. Use simple language to explain to your child what an emergency is. Describe scenarios where it is appropriate to call for help, such as when someone is hurt, there is a fire, or there is a dangerous situation. Emphasize that emergencies are serious and require immediate assistance from trained professionals.

Create age-appropriate scenarios and role-play them with your child. Pretend to be in different emergency situations and guide your child on when and how to contact emergency services. Make it interactive and encourage them to pretend to dial the emergency number on a toy phone or use imaginary play to reinforce their understanding. Utilize visual aids, such as posters or flashcards, that display the emergency numbers and symbols associated with emergency services (e.g., a picture of an ambulance or firetruck). Place these visuals in visible areas of your home, like the refrigerator or near the phone, to serve as a reminder.

Teach your child to listen to and trust adults in emergency situations. Emphasize that if they are ever in doubt or feel scared or unsafe, they should find a trusted adult and ask for help. Explain that adults are there to protect and keep them safe. Help your child learn their own full name, address, and phone number. This information can be vital for emergency services to locate them quickly. Practice saying and memorizing this information together in a fun and playful manner. It often helps to make a phone number into a jingle or a song as children can recall these so quickly.

Talk to your child about specific situations where it is appropriate to contact emergency services. For example, if someone is unconscious, there is a fire, or someone is in immediate danger. Explain that calling emergency services should be a last resort and only done in genuine emergencies. Create an environment where your child feels comfortable discussing their concerns and asking questions about emergencies. Encourage them to communicate any fears or uncertainties they may have. Assure them that it's essential to reach out for help when they genuinely need it. While teaching your child about emergency services, it's crucial to closely supervise their access to phones or other devices that can contact emergency services. Make sure they understand that calling emergency services without a genuine emergency is not appropriate.

Learn How To Dial A Number

Teaching your 2-3-year-old child your emergency contact numbers is an important safety measure. Children learn through repetition, so make it a habit to repeat the emergency contact numbers regularly. Say the numbers out loud in a clear and concise manner, emphasizing each digit. You can incorporate this into your daily routine, such as during bath time, mealtime, or before bedtime. Turn to learn emergency contact numbers into a game. Use toy phones or pretend play to simulate an emergency scenario. Encourage your child to "dial" the numbers and practice saying them aloud. You can also use playtime to reinforce the numbers by asking them to "call" you or another family member using emergency contact numbers.

Incorporate Visual Aids

Visual aids can help reinforce the numbers in your child's mind. Create a simple poster or flashcard displaying the emergency contact numbers. Use bright colors and big fonts to make it visually appealing. Hang the poster in a visible area, such as on the fridge or near their play area. Transforming the numbers into a catchy song can make learning more engaging and fun for your child. Create a simple tune using the emergency contact numbers and sing it together. Repetition combined with a melody can help them remember the numbers more easily.

Use the Power of Mnemonics

Mnemonics are potent tools that can enhance your child's memory and make learning more enjoyable. To help your child remember numbers, create simple rhymes or associations that make the information stick. For instance, for the number sequence "9-1-1", for the emergency services in the USA you can create the rhyme, "Dial Nine-One-One, Help Has Begun". Or "Nine, Nine, Nine to Save

Time" for the UK's "999" emergency number. These catchy phrases not only makes the numbers more memorable but also adds an element of playfulness to the learning process, especially when covering serious situations and not wanting to scare the children, just prepare them just incase.

When creating mnemonics, it's essential to use language and concepts that are appropriate for your child's age and comprehension level. Keep the rhymes or associations simple and easy to understand, ensuring that your child can quickly grasp and recall them. By incorporating mnemonics into their learning, you provide them with valuable tools to remember numbers and other information, fostering their cognitive development and making the learning experience more engaging and fun.

Don't Forget Positive Reinforcement

Praising and rewarding your child's efforts when they make progress or demonstrate their knowledge of emergency contact numbers is a fantastic way to encourage their learning and boost their confidence. Positive reinforcement acts as a powerful motivator and reinforces their behavior, making them more likely to continue their efforts. When your child shows their understanding of the numbers, make sure to offer genuine praise, acknowledging their achievements and efforts. A warm hug, a high five, or a word of encouragement can go a long way in boosting their self-esteem and fostering a positive attitude toward learning.

Practice in Real-Life Scenarios

To reinforce your child's understanding of emergency contact numbers, engaging in real-life scenarios and role-playing can be highly effective. Create situations where your child might need to use emergency contact numbers, such as pretending to be lost in a store or needing assistance at home. Walk them through the process of dialing the numbers and speaking to an imaginary emergency operator. This hands-on practice allows them to apply their knowledge in a practical context, enhancing their understanding and building their confidence in using emergency contact numbers.

During these role-playing sessions, provide guidance and support as needed, emphasizing the importance of staying calm and clearly communicating their situation. Encourage them to use the correct phrases and ask for help. By actively participating in these scenarios, your child gains valuable experience and develops a better grasp of how to use emergency contact numbers effectively. This practice helps build their confidence and prepares them to handle potential emergency situations with a greater sense of readiness and understanding.

Keep it Age-Appropriate

When teaching children at a young age about emergency contact numbers, it's crucial to consider their limited attention spans and developing cognitive abilities. Keep the lessons short, simple, and age-appropriate to make sure they can grasp the fundamental concept. Focus primarily on teaching them the numbers themselves, emphasizing repetition and recognition. You can incorporate visual aids, such as flashcards or posters, to help them associate the numbers with the corresponding emergency services.

Review Regularly

Continuously reviewing the emergency contact numbers with your child is a crucial step in reinforcing their knowledge and ensuring long-term retention. Make it a part of your routine to practice and refresh your memory of the numbers periodically. You can incorporate this review during daily activities or at specific times, such as during family discussions about safety or as a part of regular family meetings.

During these review sessions, engage your child in interactive activities that involve recalling the numbers. For example, you can play a memory game where you say a number, and your child has to repeat it back to you. Alternatively, you can create flashcards or a chart with emergency contact numbers and have your child identify the correct number when prompted. By incorporating these review activities into your regular routine, you provide consistent reinforcement and strengthen your child's memory of the emergency contact numbers.

Remember to be patient and encouraging during the review process. If your child struggles to recall a number, offer gentle prompts or cues to help them. Celebrate their successes and progress, and reinforce the importance of knowing these numbers for their safety. Through continuous review and reinforcement, you can make sure that your child retains and internalizes the emergency contact numbers, empowering them to respond effectively in case of an emergency.

Feelings and Emotions at a Young Age

Children who learn emotional intelligence and develop a tendency to process emotions during the early years of their childhood tend to grow up as more secure and confident adults. Understanding their own emotions and the feelings of those around them helps children develop emotional awareness, enabling them to recognize and understand their own feelings. This leads to better self-regulation as children learn to manage their emotions and make appropriate choices. It also fosters empathy and effective communication with others. Emotional intelligence contributes to long-term mental health and well-being.

By helping children identify and express their emotions, parents create a safe and open environment where children can freely communicate their feelings. Using age-appropriate language and visual aids, parents can teach children about different emotions and validate their experiences. Modeling emotional expression and problem-solving skills, as well as practicing empathy, further supports children's emotional development. Through these efforts, parents lay the foundation for their children to navigate their feelings, build healthy relationships, and enhance their overall well-being. That is why in this chapter, we are going to learn different techniques to help our children understand emotions and develop a mechanism for processing them.

Effective Communication skills

The very first step in this process is to establish a two-way communication channel between you and your children. Once you master the art of communicating with your little ones and teach them practical ways to communicate their feelings to you, the rest will become easier. To do so, start by establishing an environment where your child feels comfortable expressing their thoughts and opinions. Encourage open communication by actively listening and responding to their ideas and questions without judgment. After establishing a safe environment, here is how you can help them develop strong and practical communication skills.

Use open-ended questions

Instead of asking yes-or-no questions, use open-ended questions to encourage your child to think and express themselves. For example, instead of asking, "Do you want this toy?" you could ask, "What do you like about this toy?" Such questions will help your kid explore his own creative thinking, and his response will reflect his emotions. You can practice it by asking about other things as well, like their favorite cartoon characters, their favorite color or their clothes or food, etc.

Reflect and expand on their responses.

When your child expresses their wants or needs, reflect back on what they said to show that you are listening and understanding. Expand on their responses by asking follow-up questions or making comments that encourage them to think deeper. For example, if your child says they want ice cream, you could ask, "What flavor of ice cream do you like best?" Such questions enable them to reflect back.

Encourage decision-making

Give your child opportunities to make decisions within appropriate boundaries. For instance, you could let them choose between two snack options or decide which color crayon to use for their drawing. This helps them develop their decision-making skills and boosts their confidence. Taking your little ones shopping and asking them to pick between two sets of options will not only boost their confidence but also help develop a sense of responsibility in them.

Respect their choices

It's imperative to respect your child's choices, even if they differ from your own preferences. This means that even if you see them choosing the weirdest combination of clothes to dress up in or coloring the sky pink, just let them do that. Validate their decisions and show them that their thoughts and opinions matter. This encourages them to think for themselves and express their individuality. Instantly interrupting kids can shatter their confidence. If you want them to make a more informed choice, then model it in front of them, they eventually learn it all.

Discuss consequences

As your child expresses their wants or needs, engage them in conversations about the consequences of their choices. For example, if they want to go to the park, discuss how it might make them happy and tired. This helps them understand cause-and-effect relationships and develop critical thinking skills.

Use storytelling and play.

Kids of this age group have an attention span of 2-3 minutes, so you cannot expect them to listen with complete concentration. That is not going to happen; you will have to use other methods to engage them. Incorporate storytelling and pretend play to explore different scenarios related to wants and needs. Create characters and situations that allow your child to think about different perspectives, problem-solving, and decision-making.

Encourage imaginative thinking

Support your child's imaginative thinking by asking them questions that encourage them to think outside the box. For instance, you could ask, "If you could have any superpower, what would it be and why?"

Celebrate and appreciate their ideas.

When children are learning, every little milestone they achieve is worth all the appreciation. This positive reinforcement is essential to boost their confidence. So, show enthusiasm and appreciation for your child's ideas, no matter how simple they may seem. Celebrate their creativity and independent thinking, which will encourage them to continue expressing themselves.

Let me remind you that the success of this whole process relies highly on your level of patience, your personal understanding of your kid's psyche, and your own communication skills. So while you work on your kid, make sure to constantly keep yourself updated with the latest information, improve the communications skills that you think you might lack, and work on them.

Talk About Needs to Encourage Expression and Thinking

It is essential to understand that when kids explore and express their wants and needs, they gain a deeper understanding of themselves. This self-awareness allows them to make intelligent decisions. It also promotes reflection, analysis, and critical thinking. This process cultivates independent thinking and the ability to make choices that resonate with one's authentic self. Articulating desires and requirements helps kids develop assertiveness, active listening, and empathy. It enables them to engage in constructive communication and build healthier relationships. The question is how do you tell a two years old toddler to express their needs. Right? Well, it's true that kids cannot share their needs as we do, but we can provide them with the means and guidance to accomplish that.

Since verbal skills may still be developing at this age, encourage non-verbal communication. Help them understand that gestures, facial expressions, and body language can be powerful tools for expressing their wants and needs. Pay attention to their cues and respond accordingly. When communicating with the little ones, use simple and straightforward language. Speak in a way that they can easily understand, using sentences and vocabulary appropriate for their age. Stick to words and phrases they are familiar with, so they can confidently express themselves.

Offering choices is a great way to empower these young minds. Give them options between two or three things whenever possible. Whether it's choosing between an apple or a banana or deciding on a blue shirt or a red shirt, this practice allows them to practice decision-making and express their preferences. Visual cues can also be incredibly helpful. Utilize pictures or drawings as aids to assist children in communicating their wants and needs. Creating a visual chart or a picture board displaying everyday objects, activities, or emotions can provide a platform for them to express themselves more easily.

Being an attentive listener is crucial. Show genuine interest in what the child is trying to communicate. Get down to their eye level, maintain eye contact, and actively listen to their attempts at expressing themselves. This not only encourages them to continue expressing themselves but also helps build their confidence. Continuously validate and respond to their efforts. Even if their words may not be clear, acknowledge their attempts and validate their feelings. By doing so, you reinforce their self-expression and encourage further communication. Repeat and expand on their words or phrases to confirm understanding and stimulate their speech development. Use more descriptive words and provide additional information. For example, if they say "ball," you can respond with something like, "Yes, you want to play with the blue ball." This helps expand their language skills.

Lastly, provide a rich language environment. Surround the child with opportunities for language-rich experiences. Read books together, sing songs, and engage in conversations. This exposure to a variety of words, sentence structures, and communication styles fosters language development.

Managing emotions

By helping children recognize and express their emotions while teaching them how to regulate extreme emotions, we equip them with valuable life skills. This not only enhances their emotional well-being but also fosters healthier relationships and minimizes disruptive behavior that can result from unmanaged emotions. Start by teaching children about different emotions and helping them recognize and label their own feelings. Use age-appropriate books, visual aids, or even facial expressions to illustrate various emotions such as happiness, sadness, anger, or frustration. Encourage them to identify and express how they feel in different situations.

Expand their emotional vocabulary by introducing new words that describe nuanced feelings. Help them understand that there are different levels and variations of emotions. For example, instead of just saying "mad," they can learn words like "frustrated," "irritated," or "disappointed" to express specific emotional states. This empowers them to articulate their emotions more accurately. Show them what each emotion might look like and explain each emotion in detail through the use of visual aids like colorful emojis drawn on paper or through story characters.

Children at this age mostly learn by observing the behavior of adults and caregivers around them. You may not think that your two years old is observing you, but our little ones are great observers, and they notice everything. So, make sure to be a positive role model by demonstrating healthy ways to manage emotions. Avoid shouting in anger in front of them and show them how to calm down when feeling upset or angry, such as taking deep breaths or stepping away from a challenging situation. Practice self-regulation techniques together, and they will learn valuable strategies by example.

Introduce age-appropriate coping strategies that help children manage and regulate their emotions. These can include techniques like counting to ten, engaging in physical activities like jumping or dancing to release excess energy or engaging in calming activities like deep breathing exercises, drawing, or listening to soothing poems or music. Help them identify strategies that work best for them individually. Encourage children to find constructive solutions to situations that trigger extreme emotions. Teach them problem-solving techniques like identifying the problem, brainstorming possible solutions, and evaluating the consequences of each option. This empowers them to take control of their emotions and find proactive ways to address challenging situations. At this age, you have to lay out this whole problem, solution, and evaluation roadmap for them. Explain to them that if they are feeling anger, and they will respond in different ways, each of them will have different consequences. This technique won't show instant results as kids of this age cannot possibly follow through, but it does help lay the foundation of critical thinking in your kid, which you can work on in the years to come.

Structure and predictability in daily routines can provide a sense of security for children. Knowing what to expect and having a consistent schedule can help reduce anxiety and prevent meltdowns triggered by unexpected changes. Clearly communicate any upcoming changes and prepare them in advance to minimize emotional disruptions.

Learning Good Manners

During these early years, it is essential to foster empathy in children by teaching them to consider other people's perspectives and emotions. We can help them understand that everyone experiences a range of feelings and that their actions can impact others. We can make them engage in different activities that promote empathy, such as sharing, taking turns, or role-playing, helping children develop emotional awareness and considerate behavior. Before trying the following techniques, make sure to model good manners and empathy in your own behavior. Be polite, use kind words, and show respect and consideration towards others when you are around your children.

Courtesy Words: Start by introducing the essential courtesy words like "please," "thank you," and "sorry." Teach your child how to greet others politely, such as saying "hello" or waving when they meet someone new. Role-play different scenarios to practice greetings. Explain the importance of these words and encourage your child to use them in appropriate situations. It would greatly help you to show them when to speak those words. You can model this behavior to help them understand the concept behind the use of those words.

Role-playing: The technique that I have found most effective is role-playing. You can do that by engaging the children in pretend play scenarios where you can demonstrate and practice good manners. Use dolls or soft toy animals to act out situations that require manners, such as greeting someone, saying goodbye, or sharing. Show them that their toys are exchanging words like sorry, thank you, and please. You can also sing those words in a poem to help the children learn them quickly.

Praise positive behavior: It's very crucial to reinforce their learned behavior by offering praise. When your child exhibits good manners or shows empathy, praise and acknowledge their efforts. Positive reinforcement will motivate them to continue practicing these behaviors. When you praise them in front of others, this act will encourage them to show more kindness and good behavior toward others.

Read books about manners and emotions: One of the easiest methods to introduce good manners to your little one is the old-school "bedtime reading." These stories really create a lasting impact on a child's mind, so make sure to choose age-appropriate books that teach manners and emotional awareness. Reading together can help children understand these concepts in a fun and engaging way.

Encourage apologies: Teach your child to apologize when they have done something wrong or hurt someone's feelings. Help them understand the impact of their actions and guide them in offering a sincere apology. Again, you can use their toys to teach them the lesson on apologies. Or ask them to say sorry to your pet if they do something hurtful toward them. Create small scenarios in front of them in which you can apologize to any other member of the family for doing anything hurtful just so your child gets the idea of apologizing. And while you teach your kid how to apologize, also teach him to forgive when someone else apologizes.

Interacting with other children

During this stage, children are gradually transitioning from solitary play to more interactive play experiences. While children can interact with each other independently, it's essential for adults to provide supervision and guidance during their interactions. You, as an adult, can model positive social behaviors, offer support during conflicts, and teach appropriate ways of interacting and communicating with others. Let me explain how!

Sharing is Caring!

While sharing and turn-taking can be challenging for young children, it's crucial to introduce and encourage these skills. At this age, children are starting to grasp the concept of taking turns and sharing toys or materials. Encourage them to share and wait for their turn, fostering cooperation and empathy.

Parallel Play

At this age, children often engage in parallel play, where they play alongside each other but not necessarily together. Encourage this type of play by providing opportunities for children to engage in similar activities and observe their peers. Gradually, they may start to interact and initiate play together. You can arrange play activities for them that naturally would encourage them to share and turn-taking. For example:

Tea Party or picnic: Set up a tea party or picnic where children take turns pouring tea or serving food to their peers.

Building together: Offer toys or materials that require sharing, such as building blocks, art supplies, or puzzles. Encourage children to take turns using them and engage in cooperative play.

Teach and Reinforce the Concepts:

Use simple and age-appropriate language to explain the concepts of sharing and taking turns. Keep your instructions clear and concise. Reinforce these concepts through repetition and positive reinforcement. Use phrases like "It's Johnny's turn now, and then it will be your turn" or "Let's share the toys so everyone can play." Praise and acknowledge children when they exhibit sharing behavior or take turns appropriately.

Use Visual Aids:

Visual aids, such as pictures or charts, can be helpful in reinforcing the concepts of sharing and taking turns. You can create simple visuals with images or drawings that depict children engaging in cooperative play and sharing. Point to the visuals and use them as visual cues during playtime to remind children about sharing and taking turns. Encourage children to refer to the visuals and make connections between the images and their own behaviors.

Cooperative Games

Introduce simple cooperative games that require teamwork, sharing, and turn-taking. For example, play games like "Duck, Duck, Goose" or "Ring Around the Rosie," (or Roses for the British audience) where children take turns participating and cooperating. Engage in activities that involve passing a ball or an object to each other, encouraging children to share and take turns in the process.

At this age, it's common for young children to experience conflicts or disagreements during play. Encourage them to find peaceful resolutions by using words, expressing their feelings, and understanding different perspectives. Help them develop problem-solving skills, such as taking turns or finding compromises, to resolve conflicts in a fair and respectful manner. Remember, developing social skills and empathy takes time, practice, and patience. Be consistent in your approach and provide plenty of opportunities for children to interact with their peers. Celebrate their efforts and progress along the way, and acknowledge their positive behaviors to reinforce their understanding of sharing and taking turns.

Learning Early Motor Skills

By engaging in physical activities, children strengthen their muscles and improve their coordination. It's like a superpower for their bodies! Not only does it help them walk, run, and climb, but it also boosts their brainpower. When they crawl or walk, they explore their surroundings and become little problem solvers. Plus, have you ever seen how excited they get when they catch a ball? That's because their hand-eye coordination is getting better, and it's a skill they'll use in many activities throughout their lives. As they master these skills, they become more independent and confident, which is so important for their self-esteem. Imagine how proud they'll be when they can dress themselves or use utensils like pros! They'll feel like superheroes! And guess what? These skills also help them make friends and play with others. So, let's encourage them to play, explore, and have fun as they develop their motor skills. It's a journey that will benefit their emotional well-being, prepare them for school, and set them up for a lifetime of success!

Fine Motor Skills:

Such skills are connected to the coordination of small muscles in the body, especially the coordination of hands and fingers. These skills are crucial for tasks like holding utensils, writing, drawing, and self-care activities. Here are some ways to promote fine motor skill development:

Art and Craft Activities: Provide opportunities for children to engage in arts and crafts, such as coloring, cutting with child-safe scissors, finger painting, and using play dough. These activities help strengthen hand muscles and improve hand-eye coordination.

Sorting and Manipulating Objects: Provide various toys and objects like building blocks, puzzles, and stacking toys that require manipulation and hand-eye coordination. Encourage children to sort objects by shape, size, or color, which helps refine their fine motor skills.

Play with Manipulative Tools: Introduce children to child-friendly tools like large beads, lacing cards, and pegboards. These activities promote hand and finger dexterity and enhance their ability to grasp, manipulate, and control objects.

Sensory Play:
Sensory play engages multiple senses and is beneficial for children's overall development, including their motor skills. Remember to provide a safe and supervised environment during all these activities, ensuring that the materials and toys used are age-appropriate and

free from any potential hazards. By incorporating these strategies and activities, you can actively support the development of motor skills in 2-3-year-old children while fostering their curiosity, creativity, and physical abilities. Here are some sensory play ideas to enhance motor skills:

Sand and Water Play: Provide opportunities for children to play with sand and water using containers, scoops, and sieves. This tactile play helps develop their hand strength and finger coordination.

Play with Playdough: Allow children to explore and manipulate play dough, squeezing, rolling, and shaping it with their hands. This activity enhances finger dexterity and strengthens hand muscles.

Sensory Bins: Create sensory bins with materials like dried beans, rice, or kinetic sand, and add small toys to discover. This encourages fine motor exploration and sensory integration.

Dressing Up/Role Play:
Create a dress-up box or corner with a variety of costumes, hats, and props. Encourage children to choose and wear different outfits, pretending to be characters like superheroes, doctors, or princesses. Set up a dramatic play area with child-sized furniture, dolls, stuffed animals, and pretend-to-play items like a kitchen or a toolset. Join them in imaginative play, acting out scenarios, or engaging in pretend tea parties or construction play. Use simple props like scarves, cardboard boxes, or puppets to encourage storytelling and dramatic play. You can provide a prompt or theme and let children use their imagination to act it out.

Drawing:

Provide age-appropriate art supplies such as crayons, washable markers, and large paper. Let children explore and experiment with different colors and shapes. Offer various drawing prompts like animals, shapes, or familiar objects to spark their imagination. Encourage them to draw freely and express their ideas or feelings. Engage in collaborative drawing activities by taking turns adding elements to a communal drawing. This promotes social interaction and creativity.

Singing And Making Musical Noises:

Sing nursery rhymes, children's songs, or action songs together. Incorporate simple actions or movements to make it interactive and engaging. Provide child-friendly musical instruments like shakers, drums, or xylophones. Encourage children to explore making sounds and rhythms with the instruments. Play music from different genres and styles. Dance and move together, imitating the music or creating their own dance moves.

Jigsaw Puzzles:

Jigsaw puzzles not only enhance problem-solving skills in children of this age but they also improve hand-eye coordination, while creating spatial awareness in the child. To make them play with puzzles start with simple and age-appropriate puzzles with larger pieces. Sit with the child and guide them through the process of assembling the puzzle. Gradually introduce puzzles with more pieces or different levels of difficulty as the child progresses. Celebrate their achievements and offer encouragement as they complete each puzzle.

Gross Motor Skills:

These skills help the child use his large muscle groups. Engaging 2-3-year-old children in running, jumping, climbing, and catching activities is an excellent way to promote their gross motor skills, coordination, and physical development. Here are some ways to help children develop their gross motor skills:

Outdoor Play: Encourage outdoor playtime to provide ample opportunities for children to engage in activities like running, jumping, climbing, and playing with balls. These activities help develop their coordination, balance, and strength.

Obstacle Courses: Set up simple obstacle courses in safe environments using cushions, hoops, cones, and tunnels. This encourages children to crawl, climb, and jump, enhancing their gross motor skills while having fun.

Dance and Movement: Engage children in music and movement activities that involve dancing, hopping, marching, and stretching. This not only promotes physical coordination but also enhances their sense of rhythm and body awareness.

Running:

Create a mini "obstacle course" in a safe and open area, including cones, hula hoops, and tunnels. Guide the children through the course, allowing them to run and maneuver around the obstacles. Play games like "Follow the Leader," where you lead the children in running movements such as jogging, skipping, or hopping. Organize a simple relay race where children take turns running short distances, passing a baton (which could be a soft toy) to their teammates.

Jumping:

Set up a small obstacle course with stepping-stones or cushions that children can jump on. Encourage them to jump from one to the other, ensuring they land safely. Play games like "Jumping Jacks" or "Simon Says," incorporating jumping movements into the instructions. Provide a mini trampoline or a large cushion to jump on, ensuring appropriate safety measures.

Climbing:

Visit a playground with climbing structures suitable for young children. Supervise and assist them as they climb up ladders, stairs, or low platforms. Create a climbing area indoors using soft mats, cushions, or climbing toys like a foam climber. Allow children to explore climbing in a safe and supervised environment. Set up a crawling tunnel or a low balance beam for children to navigate and climb over.

Catching:

Start with soft and lightweight balls or beanbags that are easy for young children to catch. Toss the balls gently, encouraging them to use their hands to catch or hold them. Play games like "Catch the Balloon" or "Catch and Throw" using soft balls or scarves. Make it fun by varying the height and speed of throws. Use a parachute or a large piece of fabric to create a gentle up-and-down motion, allowing children to try catching and grasping objects as they fall from the parachute.

Make sure to provide constant supervision and ensure the environment is safe for these activities. Be patient and offer support as children develop their skills, allowing them to progress at their own pace. By engaging them in running, jumping, climbing, and catching activities, you provide opportunities for them to explore their physical abilities while promoting their overall development.

Section 2: Age 4-6 Years Old

Developing Life Skills In Everyday Tasks

Entering into this age group is an important milestone for children as they enter a new stage of development and prepare for formal schooling. During this period, children experience significant growth in various aspects of their lives. Physically, they become more coordinated and independent in their movements, allowing them to engage in more complex physical activities. Cognitive development also accelerates, with increased language skills, problem-solving abilities, and a growing capacity for logical thinking. Socially and emotionally, children start to develop a greater sense of empathy, form friendships, and navigate more complex social interactions.

However, this transition also comes with its share of challenges for both children and parents. As children gain more independence, they may face new expectations and responsibilities, which can sometimes lead to frustration and tantrums. They may also experience separation anxiety when starting school or being away from their parents for longer periods. Parents, on the other hand, need to navigate their child's increasing desire for autonomy while providing appropriate guidance and support. It can be a balancing act to encourage independence while still offering a secure and nurturing environment.

Despite the challenges, this transitional period also presents exciting opportunities for parents to explore. It is a time for parents to foster their child's curiosity and love for learning by engaging in age-appropriate activities, such as reading together, encouraging imaginative play, and providing opportunities for problem-solving and decision-making. Parents can also support their child's social development by facilitating playdates and encouraging cooperative play. Additionally, this is an ideal time to introduce routines and structures that promote self-discipline and responsibility, setting a foundation for future success.

Self-Care

Teaching self-care at this age is crucial as it empowers them with lifelong skills for physical and emotional well-being. By fostering habits such as proper hygiene, dressing themselves, and managing their emotions, children develop a sense of independence, responsibility, and self-confidence. Learning self-care at an early age lays the foundation for a healthy lifestyle and equips them with essential skills to take care of themselves, promoting their overall growth and development.

Bathing:

First things first, convincing a 4-5-year-old that bathing is a necessary part of life can be quite the challenge. They may have a natural aversion to water, akin to a cat's aversion to baths. So, we need to become skilled negotiators and expert persuaders. To decide how often they should bathe, it's best to establish a routine that works for both of you. Daily baths might turn into a battleground, with protests and slippery escapes from the tub. So, let's aim for a compromise, like every other day or a few times a week. Of course, you'll need to adjust based on their activities and how much they've managed to cover themselves in dirt and sticky substances.

Now, the art of washing. Show them that soap and water are a dynamic duo that fights off dirt and germs like superhero partners. Encourage them to get creative with bubbles and foam, turning their body into a canvas for temporary sudsy masterpieces. Teach them the importance of washing all those nooks and crannies, including behind the ears, between the toes, and those little fingers that tend to find their way into everything.

Drying off is a whole other adventure. Explain that towels are magical creatures that have the power to make us warm and cozy after a bath. Demonstrate the proper technique of towel wrapping, turning them into human burritos for ultimate snuggles. Of course, they might decide that towel origami is their newfound passion and start crafting unique towel sculptures instead.

Now, the crucial step of hanging up the towel. This is where organization and responsibility come into play. Teach them that a towel needs a designated spot, like a hook or a towel rack, to call home. Make it a game, challenging them to hit the target and score points for successful towel landings. Of course, you might find towels hanging from doorknobs, curtain rods, or even the family pet, but hey, creativity knows no boundaries!

Remember, for this age group, repetition, and gentle reminders are key. They might need occasional guidance and encouragement to embrace these self-care habits fully. So, bring out your best cheerleader spirit, celebrate small victories, and turn this learning process into a bubbly, towel-wielding adventure that leaves both of you laughing and clean!

Dressing And Undressing

Teaching young children how to dress and undress is an important skill that helps them develop independence and self-care abilities. Exploring different fastenings such as buttons, zips, Velcro, and laces can be a fun and engaging way to introduce these concepts to 4-5-year-olds. Here are some suggestions on how to teach dressing and undressing using different fastenings:

Buttons:
Start with larger buttons on simple garments like shirts or jackets. Show the child how to insert one button into the corresponding buttonhole and guide them through the process. Encourage them to practice buttoning and unbuttoning independently, providing assistance when needed. Gradually introduce smaller buttons and more complex garments as they become more proficient.

Zips:
Begin with a jacket or hoodie that has a large zipper. Demonstrate how to grasp the zipper pull and slide it up or down. Let the child practice zipping and unzipping the garment, assisting them as necessary. As they become more confident, introduce garments with smaller zippers or ones that require aligning the zipper teeth.

Velcro:
Choose clothing items with Velcro closures, such as shoes or jackets. Explain to the child how Velcro works by pressing the two sides

together to fasten and pulling them apart to unfasten. Encourage them to practice opening and closing Velcro fastenings independently.

Laces:

Begin by using larger, chunky laces or practice lacing on a board with pre-made holes. Teach the child the basic steps of lacing, such as crossing the laces over each other and pulling them through the holes. Guide them through the process initially and gradually let them practice on their own. Once they are comfortable with basic lacing, introduce more complex lacing patterns like tying shoelaces.

General Tips:

Use clothing items and materials that are appropriate for their age and size, ensuring they can easily manipulate the fastenings. Make it a playful and interactive experience by using colorful, child-friendly clothing items or dressing-up games. Provide plenty of positive reinforcement and encouragement throughout the learning process. Break down the steps into smaller, manageable tasks, and allow the child to practice each skill before moving on to the next. Be patient and understanding, as learning to dress and undress independently takes time and practice.

The Virtue Of "Cleaning"

Instilling the virtues of neatness and organization in children is essential, and a key aspect is teaching them to clean up after themselves. Begin by setting clear expectations about cleanliness and organization, explaining why it is important and the benefits it brings. Use age-appropriate language to ensure they understand the concepts and emphasize the importance of knowing where to find things when everything is in its place.

Make cleaning up a fun and engaging activity by turning it into a game or playing music while tidying. Introduce colorful bins, boxes, or storage containers to make organizing visually appealing. Provide positive reinforcement, praise, and rewards to motivate and encourage them in their efforts. By making the process enjoyable, children are more likely to embrace the habit of tidying up after themselves.

Break down cleaning tasks into manageable steps, focusing on one area or type of item at a time. Guide children through the process, offering clear instructions for each step. Teach them how to fold clothes by demonstrating and explaining each fold. Start with simple items like t-shirts or towels and gradually progress to more complex folding techniques. Encourage them to practice folding their own clothes, providing assistance and guidance as needed.

Create organizational systems that assign a designated place for each item or type of toy. Involve children in this process, allowing them to take ownership and pride in maintaining their belongings. Use labels or picture cues to help them identify where things belong. Teach them the importance of independently putting away their belongings after use and emphasize the ease of finding things when they are stored in their designated places.

As a role model, demonstrate tidiness and organization in your own behavior. Show children how you clean up after yourself and maintain an organized living space. Involve them in your cleaning routines, allowing them to assist and learn from you. By observing your example, children will be more likely to adopt these habits and understand their importance.

Basic Cleaning Skills

Helping them learn basic cleaning skills is important as it instills a sense of responsibility and helps them develop good habits early on. By teaching them age-appropriate tasks such as tidying up toys, making their bed, and wiping spills, children learn the importance of cleanliness and organization. These skills promote independence, contribute to a clean and orderly environment, and lay the groundwork for future self-sufficiency. Additionally, teaching basic cleaning skills fosters a sense of pride and accomplishment, boosting their self-esteem and shaping them into responsible individuals. While teaching them these skills, remember that at this age, children are still developing their fine motor skills and coordination. Be patient and offer guidance and support as needed. Encourage their independence and celebrate their achievements as they learn and practice these basic cleaning skills.

Wiping Up Spills Properly:
Explain to the child the importance of cleaning up spills promptly to prevent accidents and maintain a clean environment. Show them how to locate a clean cloth or paper towel and demonstrate the proper technique for wiping up spills. Teach them to blot or dab the spill rather than rub it, which can spread the mess. Encourage them to ask for help if the spill is large or if they are unsure about handling it independently. Provide positive reinforcement and praise when they successfully clean up their own spills.

Making the Bed:
Start by demonstrating how to make a bed using simple and clear steps. Break down the process into smaller tasks. For example, show them how to straighten the sheet, fluff the pillows and covers, and

fold any blankets. Provide guidance and assistance as they practice making their bed. Make it a daily routine by incorporating it into their morning schedule. Encourage them to take pride in a neat and tidy bed and reinforce their efforts with praise and positive reinforcement.

Visual Guides and Reminders:

Use visual aids, such as pictures or simple drawings, to show the child the steps involved in each task. Create a visual checklist or reminder near the areas where spills are likely to occur or next to their bed to serve as a visual cue and prompt them to clean up or make their bed.

Practice and Repetition:

Provide opportunities for the child to practice these skills regularly. Reinforce the importance of consistency and repetition in establishing these tasks as daily routines. Offer gentle reminders and encouragement when necessary, especially in the beginning stages.

Make it fun:

Turn cleaning tasks into a game or a fun activity to make them more engaging and enjoyable. Use playful language, sing songs, or set a timer to add an element of excitement. Consider offering small rewards or praise to motivate and reinforce their efforts.

Basic Kitchen Skills

When you teach your young ones basic kitchen skills, it introduces them to the world of food and cooking while developing essential life skills. By involving them in simple tasks like mixing, measuring, and stirring, children gain a sense of accomplishment and independence. They learn about different ingredients, nutrition, and food safety, fostering a healthy relationship with food from an early age. Basic kitchen skills also enhance their fine motor skills, and cognitive abilities as they follow steps and engage in sensory experiences. Moreover, teaching kitchen skills encourages creativity, critical thinking, and problem-solving, empowering children to make informed choices about what they eat and equipping them with practical skills they can carry into adulthood.

Spreading Butter on Bread:

Start with soft and manageable bread slices. Demonstrate how to hold a butter knife safely and how to spread the butter evenly on the bread. Guide the child's hand as they practice spreading the butter on their own slice of bread. Encourage them to start with small amounts of butter and gradually increase as they gain more confidence.

Making a Sandwich:

Begin with simple sandwiches like a jam or jelly sandwich. Show the child how to spread the desired fillings onto the bread and assemble the sandwich. Break down the steps and guide them through the process, allowing them to participate as much as possible. Let them choose their own fillings and encourage creativity in sandwich-making.

Pouring a Drink:

Use child-sized cups or pitchers that are easy to hold and pour. Teach the child how to hold the cup securely and pour a drink slowly and carefully. Start with small amounts of liquid and gradually increase the quantity as they become more comfortable. Remind them to watch the level of the liquid and stop pouring when the cup is almost full.

Helping with Meal Preparation:

Involve the child in simple meal preparation tasks like mixing, weighing ingredients, or cracking eggs (with supervision). Show them how to measure ingredients using appropriate measuring cups or spoons. Demonstrate the proper technique for mixing ingredients together, whether it's stirring, whisking, or folding. Start with tasks that are safe and age-appropriate, gradually increasing the complexity as the child gains skills and confidence.

Emphasize Kitchen Safety:

Teach the child about basic kitchen safety rules, such as using oven mitts when handling hot items, being cautious around sharp utensils, and washing hands before and after food preparation. Supervise them closely during tasks that involve potential risks, such as cracking eggs or using kitchen appliances.

Encourage Clean-up and Responsibility:

Teach the child the importance of cleaning up after themselves in the kitchen. Encourage them to wash their hands, wipe down surfaces, and put away utensils and ingredients after use. Reinforce the concept of responsibility and teamwork in maintaining a clean and organized kitchen environment.

Introduction To Setting The Table And Clearing Dishes.

Setting the table and clearing dishes is more than just a cute display of little hands placing forks and spoons in the right spots. It's an opportunity to instill a sense of responsibility and independence in these young ones. We are nurturing kitchen ninjas in the making, empowering them to contribute and take ownership within the family dynamic. Through teaching them proper table manners, we transform them into dining dynamos. Picture little Johnny, gracefully chewing with his mouth closed, skillfully using his utensils, and even politely saying "please" and "thank you." It's like witnessing a miniature James Bond navigating the social waters of sophisticated dinner parties. These invaluable skills will serve them well as they mingle with the elite or impress their future significant other's parents.

Setting The Table:
Begin by explaining the purpose of setting the table and the importance of each item. Introduce the basic table setting, including a plate, napkin, utensils, and a cup. Show the child where each item goes and describe its purpose. Demonstrate how to properly fold the napkin and place it next to the plate. Use simple and consistent language to describe the placement of items (e.g., "Fork on the left, knife on the right"). Provide visual cues, such as placemat outlines or picture cards, to help them remember the correct arrangement.

Clearing Dishes:
Teach the child the proper order of clearing dishes, which typically starts with removing used utensils, followed by plates and cups. Explain that dirty dishes should be placed on a tray or carried with care to avoid spills or accidents. Show them where to place the dirty dishes, such as in the sink or on the kitchen counter. Demonstrate how to scrape leftover food into the trash or compost bin before placing the dishes in the sink.

Establish A Routine:
Make setting the table and clearing dishes a regular part of their mealtime routine. Create a visual checklist or chart that outlines the

steps involved in setting the table and clearing dishes. Encourage consistency by having the child engage in these tasks during every meal.

Role-Play And Pretend-Play:

Engage the child in role-playing scenarios where they can pretend to be a waiter or host, setting the table for imaginary guests. Use play kitchen sets or toy dishes to simulate real-life table setting and clearing activities. Make the activity enjoyable and interactive to foster their engagement and learning.

Reinforce Table Manners:

Use this opportunity to reinforce basic table manners, such as sitting properly, using utensils correctly, and chewing with their mouth closed. Explain the importance of being respectful and considerate during mealtime.

Encourage your child to actively participate in setting the table and clearing dishes during meal times. Offer guidance and supervision as they learn and practice these tasks. Provide positive reinforcement and praise for their efforts to boost their confidence and motivation. Remember to be patient and provide guidance as children develop these skills. Celebrate their progress and accomplishments, and reinforce positive behavior and effort. With practice and consistent reinforcement, children will become more capable and confident in setting the table and clearing dishes.

Learning Basic Technology

The children of this era are born with a deep fascination with technology; no matter how hard you will try to keep them away from tablets, mobile phones, or laptop screens, they will be ultimately exposed to the screens at some point. So let's throw the point of "not letting them use the technology at all" out of the window and focus on how to manage their screen and how to introduce them to the technology in a way that is both helpful and controlled according to their age. I believe that by introducing them to technology at an early age, we empower them to navigate and adapt to the increasingly digital world around them. Basic technology skills, such as operating a tablet or computer, using age-appropriate educational apps or websites, and understanding the fundamentals of digital communication, lay the foundation for their digital literacy and technological fluency. These skills not only enhance their educational journey but also foster creativity, critical thinking, problem-solving, and collaboration. The question is, how can you help them learn the basic use of technology at this age? Well, here are some steps that you can take!

Step 1: Introduce Age-Appropriate Educational Games:
Select educational games that are specifically designed for their age group. Look for games that promote skills like letter recognition, counting, problem-solving, memory, or creativity. Choose games that are engaging, interactive, and have clear learning objectives.

Step 2: Teach Mouse Skills:
If using a computer with a mouse, teach them how to hold the mouse properly and move it across the screen. Guide them on how to click and drag objects using the mouse. Start with simple mouse activities like clicking on objects or dragging and dropping shapes.

Step 3: Teach Touch Screen Skills:
If using a touch screen device, explain how to navigate and interact with the screen using their fingers. Show them how to tap, swipe,

and drag objects on the screen. Teach them to use multiple fingers or gestures if the games require it.

Step 4: Set Screen Time Limits:

Teach children the importance of moderation and setting limits on screen time. Establish clear rules and boundaries for when and how long they can engage in screen activities. Use visual cues like a timer or an alarm to help them understand and manage their screen time. Model this time limit in front of them and show them how you would stop using the tablet or mobile phones after a certain time. Elaborate on this action and show them the value of limiting screen time while doing that.

Step 5: Combine Screen Time With Other Activities:

Encourage children to engage in a variety of activities beyond screen time. Promote a balance between screen activities, outdoor play, reading, art, and social interactions.

Step 6: Play Together And Monitor Content:

Join the child while they play educational games and participate in their learning experience. Monitor the content and ensure that it aligns with their age, values, and educational goals. Use the opportunity to discuss what they are learning and reinforce key concepts.

Step 7: Ensure Safety:

Teach them about internet safety rules, such as not sharing personal information online or clicking on unfamiliar links. Explain the importance of seeking help from an adult if they come across any inappropriate content. And while you can teach the lesson on safety, make sure to install apps that are safe to use for kids of this age. It is best not to leave them with the gadget alone and instead let them use the technology under adult supervision.

Step 8: Encourage Offline Learning Activities:
Minimizing screen time is crucial for your child's mental growth. Excessive technology usage often stems from boredom, making it essential to offer engaging physical activities that divert their attention from online pursuits. Introduce a variety of non-digital learning opportunities, like puzzles, building blocks, art materials, and books, to captivate their minds. Encouraging imaginative play, problem-solving, and hands-on activities will nurture their creativity and critical thinking skills. By providing these alternatives, you can foster a healthy balance between technology and constructive real-world experiences for your child's overall development.

Value And Taking Care Of Belongings

It's the right time to teach your kids the value of their, and someone else's belongings. Trust me! Once you teach them how to take care of things, you will never have to worry about the way they behave around precious things. The first step is to start by discussing the importance of belongings and how they hold value in our lives. Help them understand that taking care of their possessions shows responsibility and helps them last longer. You can share stories or examples to illustrate the significance of valuing and keeping track of their belongings.

Next, introduce the concept of organization and storage. Show the child how to designate specific places for their toys, books, and clothes. This can be done through visual cues like labels or pictures. Encourage them to put things back in their designated places after use, emphasizing the idea of preventing items from getting lost. By teaching them how to organize and store their belongings, you empower them to maintain a tidy and clutter-free space.

Personalization is another effective approach. Involve the child in personalizing their belongings, such as letting them decorate their backpack or add stickers to their lunchbox. Additionally, using labels or name tags on items like clothing or water bottles can help identify and distinguish their belongings. Explain to them that labeling assists in recognizing their items and prevents confusion or loss. While you teach the lesson of valuing belonging, make sure to demonstrate responsible behavior by taking care of your own belongings and maintaining an organized living space. Praise and encourage the child when they demonstrate responsible behavior, such as putting away their toys or keeping their room tidy. Additionally, remind them to double-check that they have all their belongings before leaving a location or transitioning to a new activity.

Teach mindful handling to help the child understand the importance of treating their belongings with care. Show them how to carry, store, and use different items properly, such as books, toys, or electronics. Emphasize the value of gentle handling and discourage rough or careless treatment. Encourage ownership and responsibility by reminding the child that they are in charge of taking care of their belongings. Discuss the potential consequences of losing or damaging items and how it can impact not only themselves but others as well. By instilling a sense of ownership and responsibility, they will develop a greater understanding of the significance of valuing and maintaining their possessions.

What works best in this exercise is to encourage empathy and sharing. Teach your child to respect other people's belongings and the importance of asking for permission before borrowing or using someone else's items. Promote the idea of sharing and taking turns, but also emphasize the importance of returning borrowed items promptly and in good condition. This helps them develop empathy and an understanding of the value others place on their belongings.

Safety and Emergency Preparedness

If you want to instill the value and importance of safety and emergency preparedness in young children, then this is the right time to do so. It equips them with the knowledge and skills to stay safe in various situations. By educating them about fire safety, basic first aid, and personal safety rules, children develop a sense of awareness and responsibility for their well-being and that of others. They learn how to identify potential hazards, make safe choices, and respond appropriately during emergencies. Teaching them about calling for help, knowing their address and phone number, and establishing a family emergency plan empowers them to take proactive measures in times of crisis. These skills not only ensure their immediate safety but also lay the foundation for a lifetime of preparedness and resilience.

Introduction To Emergency Services:

In order to prepare a child for emergency situations, it is crucial to explain to them what emergency services are and how they can provide immediate help when needed. Start by discussing different emergency scenarios that might require calling for help, such as someone being hurt, a fire, or a serious accident. Help them understand that emergencies are situations that are dangerous or require the assistance of trained professionals.

Engaging the child in role-playing scenarios can be an effective way to practice making emergency phone calls. Pretend different emergency situations and guide them on what information to provide when making the call. Teach them to stay calm, listen carefully, and answer questions from the emergency operator. This hands-on practice will help them feel more confident and prepared for real-life situations.

It is important to teach the child the basics of using a phone, including how to unlock it, access the emergency dialer, or use a speed dial function. Show them the different parts of the phone, such as the keypad, speaker, and microphone. Demonstrate how to make an emergency call using a phone, emphasizing the importance of dialing the emergency number and waiting for the operator to answer. Teach them to stay on the line until instructed to hang up.

During emergencies, it is essential for the child to stay calm and composed. Explain the importance of remaining calm and teach them techniques like deep breathing or counting to help manage their emotions. Emphasize the need to communicate clearly by speaking slowly and providing important information, such as their name, location, and the nature of the emergency. Reinforce the idea that emergency calls should only be made in genuine emergency situations and not for play or non-emergency reasons.

While it is important to teach children how to use a phone in emergencies, their primary responsibility should be to seek help from a trusted adult if available before making the call themselves. Encourage them to remember their full name, address, and any additional emergency contact numbers to provide accurate information to the emergency operator. Regularly review and reinforce these lessons through discussions and role-playing scenarios to help the child develop confidence and understand the appropriate use of emergency services. By equipping them with these skills, we empower them to take appropriate action and potentially save lives in critical situations.

Promoting Safety Habits

Instilling safety habits in children is essential for their overall well-being and protection. By teaching them basic safety rules, such as looking both ways before crossing the street, wearing seat belts, and avoiding strangers, children develop a sense of caution and responsibility. Reinforcing habits like holding hands in public, wearing helmets while riding bikes, and using sunscreen foster a culture of safety and health consciousness. By consistently modeling and discussing safe behaviors, parents and caregivers help children internalize these habits, empowering them to make safe choices independently.

Explain the Importance of Safety:

When teaching young children about safety habits, it is crucial to use simple and age-appropriate language to convey the importance of these practices. Explaining to them that safety rules are in place to keep them and others safe and to prevent accidents or injuries is key. By emphasizing the direct connection between following safety guidelines and maintaining personal well-being, children can understand that their actions have a direct impact on their own safety as well as the safety of those around them. Instilling this understanding at an early age helps cultivate a sense of responsibility and mindfulness toward safety, empowering them to make informed choices and engage in safe behaviors throughout their lives.

Helmet Safety:

Don't just tell them how to be safe - show them how! Demonstrate how to wear and adjust a helmet properly, ensuring that it fits securely on their head. Explain that wearing a helmet serves as a protective barrier for their head, reducing the risk of serious injuries in case of a fall or accident. You can wear the helmet in front of them or make their favorite teddy bear wear their helmet to teach them the importance of it. Use the story of the teddy bear who forgot to wear the helmet, fell off the bike, and got hurt. By highlighting the direct connection between not wearing a helmet and getting hurt because of it, children can understand that it is a crucial step to ensure their safety and well-being while engaging in these activities. This knowledge empowers them to make responsible choices and prioritize their own protection when participating in outdoor activities.

Road Safety:

When teaching a child how to safely cross the road, let's make it a playful adventure! Start by teaching them the catchy mantra: "Look left, right, and left again before crossing, just like a road safety champion!" Encourage them to practice this fun routine whenever they approach a road. Make waiting for a safe gap in traffic or for the pedestrian signal to change feel like a game of "Red Light, Green Light," where they can pretend to freeze like statues on red and zoom across on green. And what's more exciting than holding an adult's hand and feeling like a trusted companion while crossing the road? Turn it into a hero-themed activity, where the child gets to be the star and the adult their steadfast ally. By incorporating role-playing and imaginative scenarios, road safety becomes an enjoyable journey filled with adventure and learning!

Seat Belt Safety:

Show the child how to fasten their seat belt, making it snug like a cozy embrace across their lap and shoulder. Imagine you're a seat belt detective, ensuring everything is secure and in place. Explain that seat belts are like protective shields that keep us safe during sudden stops or unexpected adventures on the road. Just like a reliable companion, seat belts keep us securely fastened to our seats, ensuring our safety throughout the ride. So remember, whether we're embarking on a grand journey or a simple trip, our seat belts are our dependable allies, keeping us safe and sound throughout the ride!

Water Safety:

To ensure the child's safety around bodies of water such as swimming pools, lakes, or the beach, it is essential to educate them on water safety rules. This includes explaining the importance of refraining from running or pushing near the water to prevent accidents. Emphasize the significance of staying within designated swimming areas and always swimming under adult supervision. It is crucial to teach the child basic swimming skills but also stresses the importance of never going near water without an adult present to ensure their safety. By instilling these water safety rules, children can develop a responsible and cautious attitude towards aquatic environments, reducing the risk of accidents or drowning incidents.

Fire Safety:

If you want to protect your kid against fire hazards, then this is the age at which you tell them about the importance of fire safety. Show them the pictures and objects that can pose fire hazards, such as candles, lights, and matchboxes, etc. and tell them to not to use them. Visual cards depicting the hazards of fire, like the burning of hands, can help establish the dangers of fire in young minds. At this point, you only need to teach them the basics of fire safety and to seek immediate assistance from their elders in case they discover a fire.

Stranger Danger

Stranger danger refers to the concept of teaching children to be cautious and aware of strangers in order to keep themselves safe from potential harm. It is important to teach stranger danger to kids because it equips them with the knowledge and skills to protect themselves in potentially dangerous situations. By teaching children about the concept, they learn to recognize that not all strangers can be trusted, and they develop the ability to differentiate between safe and unsafe encounters. Children are taught to avoid talking to or accepting gifts from unfamiliar individuals, as well as to seek help from trusted adults, such as parents, teachers, or police officers, if they feel uncomfortable or threatened. Teaching stranger danger helps children develop a sense of personal safety, empowering them to make informed choices and minimize potential risks when interacting with unfamiliar people. Let me break down the process of introducing your child to stranger danger in a few steps. And while you are on that, make sure to continuously reinforce the importance of stranger danger and privacy through discussions, reminders, and revisiting safety rules. Encourage open communication, trust-building, and a supportive environment where the child feels comfortable discussing their concerns or questions related to stranger danger.

Strangers Vs. Safe Adults

Explain to the child that a stranger is someone they do not know or someone they have not met with their parents or guardians present. Help them understand that not all strangers are necessarily dangerous, but it's important to be cautious and follow safety rules. While you introduce them to the concept of strangers, also introduce the idea of "safe adults." These are people in their life, such as parents, teachers, or caregivers, whom they can trust and turn to if they have any concerns or feel unsafe. Show them pictures of the people they know and can confide in. This show card can include pictures of both parents or any family elder your child feels comfortable talking to.

It's essential to teach children about stranger danger, but it's equally important to emphasize that dangerous people may not always be strangers. They can be individuals they have met before, even someone introduced by their parents, without their parents being aware of their harmful intentions. A child should trust their gut instinct, and if someone makes them feel uneasy or scared, they should confide their feelings with a trusted adult. By fostering open communication and encouraging children to listen to their inner voice, we empower them to protect themselves from potential dangers, whether from strangers or familiar faces.

Discuss Personal Information:

At this point you can teach your child his name, the home address, one phone number, and the names of his parents or guardians. Emphasize that personal information should be kept private and not shared with strangers, both online and in real life.

Establish Safety Zones:

Help the child identify safe places where they can go if they feel scared or uncomfortable, such as a designated safe spot in their home or a trusted neighbor's house. Encourage them to seek help from a safe adult if they ever find themselves in a situation where they feel threatened or uncomfortable.

Role-Play Scenarios:

Engage the child in age-appropriate role-playing scenarios where they can practice responding to strangers or uncomfortable situations. Teach them how to say "no" firmly and confidently and how to seek help from a safe adult.

Trusting Instincts:

Teach the child to trust their instincts and listen to their feelings of discomfort or unease. Encourage them to tell a safe adult if they ever encounter a situation or person that makes them feel scared or uncomfortable.

LEARNING MORE ADVANCED MOTOR SKILLS

At the age of 4-5 years, children experience significant development in their motor skills. Their hand-eye coordination and fine motor skills improve as they gain more control over their fingers and hands, enabling them to draw more detailed pictures, use scissors, and manipulate objects with greater precision. Their ability to catch and throw objects also becomes more accurate. At this age, children exhibit increased confidence and proficiency in their physical abilities, allowing them to engage in a wider range of physical activities and develop greater independence in their daily tasks.

To instill a love for exercise in a child, it is important to emphasize the benefits it brings. Explain to them that exercise keeps their body strong, healthy, and full of energy. Discuss how it can make them feel happy and improve their mood, emphasizing the positive impact it has on their overall well-being. Introduce a variety of physical activities to the child to keep them engaged and excited. Offer options such as swimming, soccer, dancing, biking, or playing in the park. Provide a range of sports equipment and toys to facilitate different types of play and exploration, allowing them to discover activities that resonate with their interests.

Encourage the child to try new activities and sports. Enroll them in taster sessions or clubs where they can experience different activities in a structured and supportive environment. By exploring a variety of options, they can find what they enjoy the most and develop a lifelong passion for it. Make exercise fun and engaging for the child. Incorporate elements of play, imagination, and excitement into their physical activities. Create obstacle courses, set up treasure hunts, or engage in playful competitions to make exercise enjoyable and something they eagerly look forward to.

How To Ride A Bike?

Teaching your child to ride a bike can be a wonderful adventure! Watching them pedal for the first time is a special memory. To make it enjoyable, give the bike a fun name, like "Zoomer" or "Adventure Express," and decorate it with colorful streamers, stickers, and a personalized nameplate. Tell your child that this bike has special powers, and when they ride it, they can go on incredible adventures to far-off lands. Children have great imaginations, so tapping into that unlocks the fun.

Before hopping on the bike, engage in activities that build balance and coordination. Set up a mini obstacle course with cones, cushions, or toys, and encourage your child to walk, hop, or tiptoe through it like they're on a daring quest. This helps them develop balance and prepares them for bike riding. Now, it's time to transform the bike into their very own adventure machine! Attach training wheels and let your child decorate them with their favorite colors or stickers, making the bike feel even more special.

Introduce safety as an essential aspect of riding a bike by creating "Safety Superheroes." Dress up with fun accessories, and assign creative names to each safety rule. For example, Helmet Hero ensures they always wear their helmet, Pad Protector encourages knee and elbow pads, and Traffic Tamer teaches road safety. Explain how these superhero rules keep them safe during their bike adventures.

When it's time to start riding, find a spacious and safe area, like a park or empty parking lot. Play games like "Follow the Leader," where you ride in front, demonstrating turning, stopping, and starting, while your child mimics your actions. This teaches the fundamentals of riding a bike while adding fun and interaction.

To make the learning experience more exciting, create a mini "Bike Safari." Set up objects or pictures around the area, and encourage your child to collect imaginary treasures or spot specific items as they ride. This playful adventure lets them explore while practicing bike skills.

As your child gains confidence, gradually remove one training wheel at a time. Explain that they're becoming more accomplished riders, and their bike is transforming into a true two-wheeled adventure machine. Celebrate each milestone with cheers and applause, boosting their confidence and motivation.

Once they become more proficient, consider organizing a small bike parade with friends or family. Dress up in fun costumes, decorate the bikes, and ride together through the neighborhood or local park. This culminating event will create a sense of accomplishment and pride for mastering this skill and making a difference.

Learning To Swim

Most kids start showing signs of loving water at this age by wanting to stay in their bathtubs and play for as long as they can. And that is your cue to officially introduce them to the concept of swimming which I must say is a great healthy activity that you can teach your kid. It greatly helps them develop good mind and muscle coordination; moreover, it also helps them overcome their fear of water or drowning. It is easier to teach swimming to kids at this age as they are more open to exploration and experience fewer fears. Here is what you can do to make them love swimming!

Water Exploration:

Start by introducing the pool as a magical and inviting place. Talk to your child about the wonders of the water and the exciting things they can do in it. Explain that they will learn to swim like a fish or mermaids, exploring the depths of the pool like brave adventurers.

Water Safety Superheroes:

Teach water safety as an essential part of swimming by creating Water Safety Champions. Give them catchy names like "Safety Captain" or "Aquatic Protector." Dress up or use pool toys as props to represent these champions. Explain how they keep us safe in and around the water by wearing life jackets, staying close to adults, and listening to safety rules.

Bubble Blowing and Underwater Exploration:

Teach your child how to blow bubbles in the water. Make it a playful activity by pretending to be underwater creatures, such as dolphins or whales, communicating through bubble signals. Encourage them to dip their faces in the water, blow bubbles, and imagine they are exploring a magical underwater world.

Floating Friends:

Introduce the concept of floating by using floatation devices or pool noodles as "Floating Friends." Explain that these friends help us stay safe and learn to float effortlessly. Create stories about these friends, such as "Floatie the Friendly Float" or "Buoyant Buddy." Encourage your child to hold onto them and experience the sensation of floating on the water's surface.

Kickboard Adventures:

Introduce a kickboard as their trusty "Kickboard Cruiser." Encourage them to hold onto it while kicking their legs, pretending they're zooming through the water like a mermaid, or racing against friendly sea creatures. This activity helps build leg strength and coordination while making swimming feel like an exciting adventure.

Water Games:

Incorporate water games into the swimming lessons to make them interactive and engaging. Play games like "Follow the Leader," where you demonstrate different swimming strokes and movements, and your child imitates them. Use colorful pool toys or dive rings to create games that involve retrieving objects from the water. These games make learning to swim a playful and enjoyable experience.

Gradual Submersion:

Help your child become comfortable with submerging their head underwater. Start by having them practice blowing bubbles and gradually progress to gentle submersion. Use colorful diving rings or toys as targets to encourage them to put their face in the water and retrieve the objects. Make it a treasure hunt and celebrate their success each time they find a "treasure" underwater.

Swim Skills Obstacle Course:

Create a swim skills obstacle course using pool noodles, floating toys, and hula hoops. Set up stations where your child can practice different skills, such as floating, kicking, or reaching for objects. Turn it into an adventure by pretending they are on a water obstacle course challenge. Celebrate their achievements as they navigate through the course.

Water Confidence and Playtime:

Dedicate a portion of each swimming session to unstructured playtime. Let your child splash, jump, and play in the water, building their confidence and comfort. Support them as they explore their own abilities and discover the joy of being in the water. Remember to always maintain close supervision for their safety.

Gradually increase the difficulty of the activities as your child becomes more comfortable and confident in the water. Celebrate their progress and achievements along the way. Plan a special swimming celebration day where family and friends can witness their swimming skills and cheer them on. Since every child is unique, you need to personalize the above-mentioned swimming regimen according to the needs of your child. If your child is hesitant to get into a pool, then start with something small like an inflated pool and allow them to naturally grow fond of water.

Introduce Letters and Numbers:

Learning letters and numbers at this age helps children develop language and communication skills. It introduces them to the building blocks of written language, allowing them to recognize and form words. Understanding them enhances their ability to express themselves, listen, and comprehend information.

Create An Alphabet Adventure:

Take your little ones on a thrilling alphabet adventure. Imagine you are explorers searching for hidden letters in your house or backyard. Encourage them to find objects that start with different letters of the alphabet. This hands-on activity makes learning letters exciting and encourages their observational skills.

Sing And Dance:

Incorporate catchy songs and lively dances to introduce letters and numbers. There are plenty of educational songs available online that can make learning more enjoyable. You can create your own tunes or use popular children's songs with modified lyrics that focus on letters and numbers. Encourage them to dance and move while singing along, making the learning experience interactive and fun.

Alphabet And Number Games:

Engage your children in various games that involve letters and numbers. For example, you can create a treasure hunt where they search for hidden letters or numbers. Use colorful cards or toys with letters and numbers printed on them and encourage them to match, sort, or stack them. These interactive games enhance their cognitive skills while keeping them entertained.

Alphabet Treasure Hunt: Hide alphabet cards around the house or outdoor area. Provide clues to guide children to find and collect the hidden letters.

Letter Matching: Create pairs of cards with uppercase and lowercase letters. Scatter them face-down on a table and have your child take turns flipping two cards at a time and find the matching letters.

Number Hopscotch: Draw a hopscotch grid on the floor or use colored tape. Children can hop on the squares in numerical order, saying the numbers out loud as they go. You could change the shape of the hopscotch course for a more exciting challenge, for example a circular hopscotch with the numbers arranged in an inward spiral direction. You could also try other shapes, especially if using chalk on the patio! Triangle, rectangle or even a rocket shaped hopscotch.

Alphabet Bingo: Create bingo cards with different letters. Call out letters randomly and have children place a marker on the corresponding letter on their bingo card. The first one to complete a row or the entire card wins.

Counting Bean Bag Toss: Set up a numbered target board using buckets or hula hoops with numbers written inside. Children can toss bean bags into the target and practice counting based on the number they land in.

Letter Scavenger Hunt: Provide children with a list of letters to find in their surroundings. They can search for objects that start with each letter or locate printed letters hidden around the room.

Number Memory Game: Take pairs of number cards ranging from 1 to 10. Shuffle them and place them face-down on a table. Now ask your child to take turns flipping two cards at a time, aiming to find matching number pairs.

Alphabet Puzzles: Use alphabet puzzles with large, chunky pieces to help children recognize and assemble letters in the correct order.

Number Fishing: Create fish-shaped cutouts with numbers written on them and attach a paperclip to each fish. Use a fishing rod with a magnetic end and have children "fish" for numbers, calling out the number they catch.

Alphabet Relay Race: Divide children into teams and provide each team with a set of letter cards. Place a basket or container at a distance from each team. Children take turns running to the basket, selecting a letter card, and bringing it back to their team. The first team to collect all the letters of the alphabet wins.

Letter And Number Art:

Incorporate art activities that involve letters and numbers. Provide them with large sheets of paper and various art supplies like crayons, markers, and stickers. Encourage them to draw or decorate the letters and numbers creatively. This allows them to associate visual representations with the corresponding symbols, making the learning process more enjoyable and memorable. You can make them color large alphabet letters or numbers drawn on paper. Add colorful images and engaging images to capture their attention.

Storytelling And Books:

Read engaging storybooks that revolve around letters and numbers. Choose colorful picture books with appealing illustrations that highlight different letters and numbers. Pause during the story and ask questions related to the characters or objects in the book. This interactive approach enhances their comprehension and reinforces letter and number recognition.

Sensory Play:

Incorporate sensory play to introduce letters and numbers. Let them trace their fingers or use play dough to mold the shapes of different letters and numbers. This tactile experience stimulates their senses and reinforces their understanding of the symbols.

Caring for Living Things

Teaching your kids to care for living things is crucial for their emotional development, environmental consciousness, and overall growth. It helps foster empathy, teaches them about responsibility and the natural world, and provides them with meaningful experiences that can enhance their well-being. By instilling these values early on, parents can empower their children to become compassionate, responsible, and caring individuals.

Caring For Plants

Plant care is important because it not only helps children learn about the natural world but also instills in them a sense of responsibility and nurturance. Plus, it's a fun and rewarding way to spend time together as a family! Remember, the key is to make plant care a positive and enjoyable experience for your child. Encourage their curiosity, answer their questions, and celebrate their efforts. By involving them in plant care from a young age, you're helping them develop valuable skills and a lifelong appreciation for nature.

Now, let's talk about some tasks that parents can help little kids do to take care of plants:

Watering: Teach your child how to water plants gently and explain that plants need water to grow. Show them how to check the soil and explain that it should be moist but not soaking wet. Let them take turns watering the plants under your guidance.

Sunshine Check: Help your child understand that plants need sunlight to make food through a process called photosynthesis. Take them outside and show them how to find a sunny spot for the plants. Encourage them to move potted plants around to ensure they get enough sunlight during the day.

Plant Observation: Spend time with your child observing the plants together. Teach them to look for changes like new leaves, flowers, or even signs of pests. Encourage them to ask questions and engage in discussions about what they observe.

Gentle Pruning: Show your child how to remove dead or yellowing leaves from the plants. Explain that pruning helps the plants stay healthy and encourages new growth. Give them child-safe scissors and let them carefully trim away the damaged parts.

Soil Care: Explain to your child the importance of good soil for plant growth. Help them loosen the soil gently with a small garden tool, like a child-sized rake or shovel. Teach them to remove any weeds they find and to add organic matter like compost or mulch to nourish the soil.

Plant Feeding: Introduce your child to the concept of plant food or fertilizer. Show them how to sprinkle a small amount of fertilizer around the base of the plants, emphasizing that it helps plants stay strong and healthy. Ensure they understand the importance of using the right amount.

Decorate the Plant Area: Let your child unleash their creativity by allowing them to decorate the plant area with colorful stones, labels, or handmade signs. This will make them feel proud of their contribution to the plants' well-being.

Caring For A Pet

Having a pet can be a wonderful and rewarding experience for children, and it's important for parents to teach kids how to care for their furry friends. Not only does it help develop a sense of responsibility, but it also nurtures empathy and companionship. Moreover, it's a fantastic way to create lasting memories and build a loving bond with the family pet!

Now, let's discuss some tasks that parents can help little 4-6-year-old kids do to take care of their pets:

Feeding: Teach your child about the importance of regular meals for pets. Show them how to measure the appropriate amount of food and help them fill the pet's food bowl. Explain that different pets have different dietary needs, and it's essential to feed them the right food.

Watering: Explain to your child that just like people, pets need fresh water to stay hydrated. Show them how to refill the water bowl or bottle, and encourage them to check it regularly. Make sure they understand that clean water is crucial for their pet's health.

Gentle Playtime: Show your child how to play with the pet in a kind and gentle manner. Teach them to respect the pet's boundaries and avoid rough or aggressive behavior. Encourage them to engage in interactive play with toys that are suitable for the pet.

Brushing and Grooming: Depending on the type of pet, introduce your child to the concept of brushing and grooming. Teach them how to use a soft brush to gently groom the pet's fur or how to help clean their feathers or scales. Emphasize that grooming keeps the pet clean and comfortable.

Cleaning Up: Explain to your child the importance of keeping the pet's living area clean. Show them how to scoop litter for cats or pick up waste for dogs. Encourage them to help with simple cleaning tasks like tidying up the pet's bedding or wiping down their toys.

Observation and Care: Teach your child to observe the pet's behavior and body language. Explain that it helps them understand if the pet is feeling happy, scared, or unwell. Encourage them to inform you if they notice anything unusual, so you can address it promptly.

Cuddles and Affection: Help your child understand the importance of love and affection for pets. Encourage them to spend quality time cuddling, petting, or simply being near their furry friend. Teach them to be gentle and respect the pet's personal space.

Keep in mind that supervision and guidance are crucial when children interact with pets. Be patient and encourage your child's involvement, making sure they understand that pets rely on them for their well-being. By teaching them these tasks, you're not only nurturing their sense of responsibility but also fostering a loving and caring relationship between your child and their pet.

Visit Farms And Zoos

Taking kids to farms and zoos can be an incredibly enriching experience for both children and parents. These outings provide wonderful opportunities for learning, exploration, and connection with the natural world. Let's explore why parents should take their little 4-6-year-old kids to farms and zoos, and the various things they can teach during these visits.

__Learning about Animals__: Farms and zoos offer a chance for children to see a wide variety of animals up close. Parents can teach kids about different animal species, their habitats, and their unique characteristics. They can share interesting facts and engage in conversations about animal behavior, diet, and conservation.

__Appreciating Biodiversity__: By visiting farms and zoos, children can witness the diversity of animal life. Parents can explain how each animal plays a vital role in maintaining balance in the ecosystem. This helps foster an appreciation for the beauty and importance of biodiversity.

__Building Empathy and Respect__: Interacting with animals encourages children to develop empathy and respect for other living beings. Parents can teach kids about treating animals with kindness, emphasizing the importance of gentle touch, appropriate behavior, and not disturbing them when they're resting or eating.

Understanding Animal Care: Farms and zoos often have educational programs or displays that show how animals are cared for. Parents can explain the role of zookeepers or farmers in ensuring the well-being of the animals. They can discuss topics like proper nutrition, shelter, and veterinary care, highlighting the responsibilities involved in animal care.

Conservation Awareness: Visiting these places provides an opportunity to discuss the importance of conservation and protecting animal habitats. Parents can explain the threats animals face in the wild and the efforts taken to preserve their environments. This helps instill a sense of responsibility and the idea that we all have a role to play in conservation.

Sensory Experience: Farms and zoos stimulate children's senses and offer hands-on experiences. Parents can encourage kids to listen to animal sounds, feel different textures, and observe colors and patterns. They can engage in sensory activities such as petting animals with adult supervision or feeding them with guidance.

Appreciating Farm Life: Farms provide insights into agricultural practices and the connection between humans and the land. Parents can teach kids about growing crops, harvesting, and caring for farm animals. They can explore concepts like where food comes from, the seasons, and sustainable farming practices.

Nature Connection: These outings allow children to spend ample time connecting with nature, away from the city life. You can teach kids about the importance of fresh air, green spaces, and the benefits of spending time outdoors. They can encourage observation of plants, flowers, and other aspects of the natural environment.

Make sure to engage in age-appropriate discussions, answer questions patiently, and encourage curiosity during these visits. By taking kids to farms and zoos, parents create memorable experiences that inspire a love for animals, nature, and conservation, setting the stage for a lifelong appreciation of the natural world.

Waste Management for a Healthier Environment

Teaching your kids about proper waste management, such as throwing trash in the bin and recycling, is essential for several reasons. By instilling these habits from a young age, parents can help their children understand the importance of caring for the environment and the well-being of living creatures. Let's explore why it's important and the different techniques parents can use to teach little 4-6-year-old kids about waste management.

Protecting Living Creatures: Explaining to children that throwing trash in the bin is crucial for the safety of living creatures helps them understand the impact of their actions. They can learn that litter left outside harms animals, who might accidentally ingest it or get entangled in it. By properly disposing of trash, children contribute to creating a safer environment for animals.

Environmental Responsibility: Teaching kids about waste management helps them develop a sense of environmental responsibility. They learn that their actions have consequences and that caring for the planet is everyone's responsibility. By recycling and throwing trash in the bin, children actively participate in protecting the Earth's resources and reducing pollution.

Now, let's explore techniques parents can use to teach little ones about waste management:

Visual Aids:

Use colorful pictures or posters to illustrate the concept of waste management. Show examples of different types of waste, such as plastic bottles, food scraps, or paper, and explain how each should be handled. Visual aids make the information more engaging and easier for children to understand.

Sorting Games:

Create a game where children sort items into different bins for trash, recycling, and composting (if applicable). Use representative objects like paper, plastic, and food waste. Encourage children to match each item to the appropriate bin, explaining the reasons behind their choices.

Storytelling:

Use age-appropriate stories or books that highlight the importance of waste management. Choose tales that emphasize the consequences of littering or the benefits of recycling. Discuss the stories with your child and ask them questions to gauge their understanding and encourage further conversation.

Role-Playing:

Engage in imaginative play where you and your child pretend to be responsible waste managers. Set up a pretend recycling station or bin, and encourage your child to sort items correctly. Make it fun by using props and incorporating dialogue to reinforce the importance of waste management.

Field Trips:

Take your child on trips to recycling centers or waste management facilities if possible. Let them observe firsthand how waste is processed and recycled. This experience can deepen their understanding and make the concept more tangible.

Lead by Example:

Children learn best by observing and imitating their parents. Make sure to demonstrate proper waste management practices in your daily life. Involve your child in tasks such as recycling, composting, or throwing trash away, and explain why you're doing it.

Reinforcement and Positive Encouragement:

Praise your child's efforts and progress in waste management. When they demonstrate proper disposal habits or show understanding of recycling, acknowledge their actions and explain why it matters. Positive reinforcement encourages them to continue practicing responsible waste management.

Teaching waste management is an ongoing process, and repetition is key. Be patient, answer their questions, and reinforce the importance of their actions. By teaching children about waste management, parents equip them with lifelong skills that promote environmental stewardship and contribute to a cleaner and healthier planet.

FEELINGS AND EMOTIONS WHEN INTERACTING WITH OTHERS

Parents absolutely need to teach their little ones about feelings and emotions when they're out and about in the world of human interaction. Why, you ask? Well, it's like giving them the tools to navigate social situations confidently! When kids understand and express their own emotions, they become socially adept with empathy, kindness, and respect. And hey, it's not just about them – it's about making the world a better place, one heartfelt connection at a time. So let's raise a bunch of emotionally intelligent young individuals who can spread harmony and inclusivity wherever they go!

Overcoming Shyness

Parents play a vital role in supporting their children to overcome shyness, as it enables them to build confidence, engage with others, and develop essential social skills that will serve them well in the future.

Shyness is a natural trait in young children as they navigate the world and learn to interact with others. Now, let's explore some friendly techniques parents can use to assist their 4-6-year-old kids in overcoming shyness:

Create a Safe and Supportive Environment: Foster an environment where your child feels safe, loved, and encouraged. Offer praise and reassurance, emphasizing that it's okay to feel shy sometimes. Be patient and understanding, allowing them to take their time to feel comfortable in social situations.

Lead by Example: Children often learn by observing their parents. Model confident and positive social interactions, such as initiating conversations, making eye contact, and displaying open body language. Let your child see you engaging with others and expressing yourself comfortably.

Practice Social Skills: Encourage your child to practice social skills through role-playing or imaginative play. Pretend to be different characters and act out social situations, like introducing themselves to new friends or ordering food at a pretend restaurant. This helps familiarize them with social interactions in a safe and fun way.

Gradual Exposure: Introduce your child to social settings gradually. Start with small, familiar gatherings or playdates with close friends. As they become more comfortable, gradually expose them to larger groups or unfamiliar situations. This progressive approach helps build their confidence over time.

Encourage Communication: Teach your child effective communication skills, such as using clear and friendly language, active listening, and asking questions. Practice these skills during everyday activities and encourage your child to express their thoughts and feelings.

Celebrate Small Victories: Acknowledge and celebrate your child's efforts and achievements when they step out of their comfort zone. Whether it's initiating a conversation or joining a group activity, praise their bravery and remind them of how proud you are. This positive reinforcement builds their confidence and encourages further growth.

Empathy and Understanding: Help your child develop empathy and understanding towards others. Teach them to recognize and appreciate different personalities and perspectives. Encourage kindness, inclusivity, and sharing, creating an atmosphere of acceptance and support.

If shyness significantly affects your child's daily life or relationships, consider consulting a professional, such as a child psychologist or therapist, who can provide specialized guidance and support.

Making Friends

You as a parent can play a vital role in teaching your kids how to make friends because friendships are an essential part of the social and emotional development of a child. Having friends at a young age helps children learn valuable skills like communication, empathy, and cooperation. It also provides them with a support system, boosts their self-esteem, and fosters a sense of belonging. Now, let's explore some friendly techniques parents can use to help their little 4-6-year-old kids make friends:

Encourage Social Interaction: Create opportunities for your child to interact with other children in different settings. Arrange playdates, enroll them in group activities or classes, and visit parks or community events where they can meet and play with new friends.

Teach Social Skills: Help your child develop basic social skills like introducing themselves, sharing, taking turns, and listening to others. Role-play social situations with them and provide gentle guidance on appropriate behaviors and positive communication.

Foster Empathy and Kindness: Encourage your child to understand and empathize with others' feelings. Teach them to be kind, considerate, and inclusive. Explain the importance of treating others with respect and how empathy strengthens friendships.

Model Friendship Skills: Demonstrate positive friendship skills through your own interactions with others. Show your child what it means to be a good friend by being kind, supportive, and a good listener. Your actions speak louder than words!

Promote Cooperative Play: Engage your child in activities that require cooperation and teamwork. Encourage them to work together with others, share toys, and take turns. Cooperative play helps children build relationships and develop problem-solving skills.

Emphasize Communication: Teach your child effective communication skills, such as using kind words, making eye contact, and listening actively. Encourage them to express their thoughts and feelings clearly and respectfully. Effective communication is essential for building and maintaining friendships.

Celebrate Individuality: Help your child embrace their uniqueness and encourage them to appreciate others' differences. Teach them that true friendships are built on acceptance and embracing diversity.

Be Patient and Supportive: Understand that making friends takes time and may involve setbacks. Be patient and supportive during the process. Encourage your child to persevere, offering guidance and reassurance along the way.

Foster Independence: Allow your child to take small steps towards making friends independently. Encourage them to approach others, initiate conversations, and invite peers to play. Offer gentle support and encouragement when needed.

Practice Active Listening: Teach your child the importance of listening attentively to others. Encourage them to ask questions and show genuine interest in their friends' thoughts and feelings. Active listening strengthens connections and fosters deeper friendships.

Enhancing Communication Skills

Parents are like communication champions in their kids' lives! They teach their little ones to speak with clarity, engage in conversations, and listen attentively. With these skills, children become confident and active participants in any chat. But remember, building these abilities takes time and practice. Be patient and provide ongoing support and encouragement. By teaching your child to speak clearly, actively listen, and engage in conversations, you equip them with invaluable tools for successful communication and meaningful connections with others. So, hold on tight as we dive into some friendly techniques parents can use to nurture the communication prowess in their adorable 4-6-year-old kiddos!

Lead by Example: Model clear and articulate speech when interacting with your child and others. Speak slowly and enunciate words, showing them how to communicate effectively. Engage in conversations with your child, demonstrating active listening by maintaining eye contact and responding attentively.

Encourage Storytelling: Create a storytelling environment where your child can practice speaking and expressing their thoughts. Encourage them to share their own stories or retell events from their day. This helps develop their language skills and boosts their confidence in speaking up.

Ask Open-Ended Questions: Encourage your child to engage in conversations by asking open-ended questions. This promotes thoughtful responses and encourages them to express their ideas and opinions. Ask questions that require more than a simple "yes" or "no" answer, allowing for richer discussions.

Active Listening Games: Play listening games with your child to improve their listening skills. You could play "Simon Says" or create a "Sound Scavenger Hunt" where they listen for specific sounds in their environment. These games help them focus and sharpen their listening abilities.

Practice Turn-Taking: Teach your child the importance of taking turns during conversations. Encourage them to listen while others speak and wait patiently for their turn to talk. This helps develop respectful communication habits and encourages active participation in discussions.

Story Retelling: After reading a story or watching a movie together, ask your child to retell the story in their own words. This exercise improves their listening comprehension and helps them organize their thoughts for clear communication.

Play "Guess the Sound": Play a game where you or your child make different sounds, and the other person guesses what it is. This activity enhances listening skills and promotes active engagement in conversations.

Create Conversation Starters: Make conversation cards with fun and interesting questions or topics. Use these cards during mealtime or family gatherings to encourage everyone, including your child, to engage in conversations and practice speaking and listening.

Provide Feedback and Praise: Offer feedback and praise when your child speaks clearly or actively listens. Point out their efforts and improvements, boosting their confidence and reinforcing positive communication habits.

Create a Safe and Supportive Environment: Foster an atmosphere where your child feels comfortable expressing their thoughts and ideas. Create a judgment-free zone where they can ask questions and voice their opinions without fear of criticism.

Section 3: Age 6-10 Years Old

Improve Reading and Communication Skills

Picture a world where your 6-10-year-olds confidently stride like mini-adults, facing life's challenges with a twinkle in their eyes and a skip in their step. How can we turn this vision into reality? By teaching them basic life skills, of course! These skills act as the secret sauce of independence and self-sufficiency. From tying shoelaces to packing their own backpacks, these little champions will be ready to conquer the world, one skill at a time. Not only does it boost their confidence, but it also instills a sense of responsibility and prepares them for the exciting adventures ahead. So, get ready to embark on this thrilling journey of empowering our 6-10-year-old wonders with the tools they need to thrive in life!

Learn To Love Reading

Reading is a wonderful and essential habit to cultivate in children. It opens a world of knowledge, sparks creativity, and helps develop vital skills such as communication, critical thinking, and empathy. As a parent, you play a crucial role in instilling a love for reading in your little ones. The key is to make reading a fun and enjoyable experience for your child. Celebrate their progress, offer praise and encouragement, and be patient. Over time, they will develop a genuine love for reading that will benefit them throughout their lives. Here are some friendly steps you can take to foster this love in your 6-10-year-old children:

Be a reading role model: Children often imitate their parents, so let them see you enjoy books. Make reading a part of your daily routine, whether it's novels, newspapers, or even magazines. Your enthusiasm will inspire them.

Create a cozy reading environment: Designate a special reading nook or a comfortable corner in your home where your child can enjoy their books. Add some soft cushions, a cozy blanket, and good lighting to create a cozy and inviting atmosphere.

Choose age-appropriate books: Select books that align with your child's interests and reading level. Look for colorful and engaging books with captivating illustrations that will grab their attention. Let them have a say in choosing books to increase their enthusiasm.

Make reading a shared activity: Set aside dedicated reading time as a family. Create a tradition where everyone gathers to read their favorite books. Take turns reading aloud or discussing the stories afterward to encourage conversation and bonding.

Visit the library or bookstore: Take your child on regular trips to the library or bookstore. Let them explore different genres and discover new books that pique their interest. Encourage them to borrow or buy books they are excited about.

Incorporate reading into daily life: Show your child that reading is not limited to books alone. Encourage them to read signs, labels, and instructions while you're out and about. Engage them in reading menus, recipes, or even grocery lists during everyday activities.

Organize a reading challenge or club: Create a reading challenge or club with your child's friends or classmates. Set goals, reward their achievements, and provide a platform for them to discuss their favorite books. This fosters a sense of community and motivates them to read more.

Embrace different reading formats: Don't limit reading to traditional books. Explore audiobooks, e-books, or interactive apps that offer engaging and interactive reading experiences. This variety can add excitement and cater to different learning styles.

How To Communicate and Write Effectively

Effective communication and writing skills are valuable assets that can unlock incredible opportunities for kids. They help them express themselves with confidence and excel in school and beyond. As a caring parent, you have the incredible power to guide your 6-10-year-old child on this exciting journey of mastering communication and writing skills. Let's embark on this adventure together and equip your little one with the essential skills they need to thrive in the world! Here are some steps you can take:

Encourage open conversation: Create an environment at home where your child feels comfortable expressing their thoughts and feelings. Listen attentively when they speak and encourage them to ask questions. This helps them develop their communication skills and builds their confidence.

Teach active listening: Maintaining eye contact, asking relevant questions while listening to someone, and providing appropriate responses, are all the major components of active listening, and we should teach those techniques to the kids as well. This fosters effective communication and shows respect for others.

Model clear and concise communication: Be mindful of how you communicate with your child. Use simple and clear language, avoiding jargon or complex terms. Model effective communication by speaking at an appropriate pace, using proper grammar, and maintaining a respectful tone.

Expand their vocabulary: Introduce new words to your child regularly. Engage in conversations that challenge their vocabulary and encourage them to use new words in their own speech. Reading books together is an excellent way to expose them to a wide range of vocabulary. Here are some engaging activities to help expand vocabulary for your kids:

- **Word of the Day:** Introduce a "Word of the Day" activity. Each day, present a new word to your child and encourage them to use it in different contexts throughout the day. Discuss its meaning, synonyms, and antonyms.

- **Vocabulary Games**: Play word-based games such as Scrabble, Boggle, or Bananagrams. These games encourage children to form words, explore new combinations, and discover unfamiliar vocabulary.

- **Storytelling and Word Building**: Engage your child in storytelling activities where they need to incorporate specific words. You can provide a list of challenging words, and they can create imaginative stories that include those words.

- **Vocabulary Journal**: Encourage your child to maintain a vocabulary journal where they write down new words they encounter. They can include definitions, example sentences, and illustrations to help them remember and understand the words better.

- **Reading Challenges**: Set reading challenges for your child, such as reading a certain number of books or completing a reading list. This exposes them to a wide range of vocabulary and encourages them to explore new genres.

- **Word Association**: Play word association games where you start with a word, and your child has to quickly come up with another word related to it. This helps them make connections and expand their vocabulary in a fun and interactive way.

- **Picture-Word Match**: Choose a set of flashcards or picture books that depict various objects or actions. Encourage your child to match the words with the corresponding pictures, reinforcing their vocabulary in a visual manner.

- **Vocabulary Charades**: Play a game of charades using vocabulary words. Your child can act out the meaning of the word without using spoken language, and you can guess the word. This activity makes learning vocabulary playful and interactive.

- **Context Clues**: While reading together, teach your child to use context clues to figure out the meaning of unfamiliar words. Discuss how the surrounding words and sentences can provide hints about the word's definition.

- **Word Puzzles:** Engage in word puzzles like crosswords, word searches, or word scrambles. These puzzles challenge your child's problem-solving skills and expose them to a range of vocabulary words.

Practice writing activities: Provide opportunities for your child to practice writing in a fun and engaging manner. Encourage them to keep a journal, write stories, or even create their own mini-books. Set aside regular writing time where they can express their thoughts freely. Here are some engaging activities to help 6-10-year-old kids practice their writing skills:

- **Story Starters:** Provide your child with a sentence or a prompt to start a story. Encourage them to continue the story and let their imagination run wild. This activity helps develop their creativity and narrative writing skills.

- **Letter Writing**: Encourage your child to write letters to friends, family members, or even fictional characters. They can express their thoughts, share experiences, or ask questions. Letter writing helps develop their communication skills and provides a meaningful purpose for writing.

- **Journaling**: Encourage your child to keep a daily journal where they can write about their thoughts, experiences, or dreams. This activity helps them practice expressing themselves and improves their writing fluency.

- **Writing Prompts**: Provide your child with interesting writing prompts, such as "If I could have any superpower, I would choose..." or "The best day of my life was when..." This stimulates their creativity and encourages them to write freely.

- **Storyboarding:** Introduce the concept of storyboarding, where your child can create a visual representation of a story or an event using pictures and captions. This activity helps them develop their storytelling skills and enhances their ability to organize ideas.

- **Collaborative Story Writing:** Engage in collaborative story writing where you and your child take turns adding sentences or paragraphs to create a story together. This activity fosters teamwork, creativity, and improves their writing skills.

- **Book Reviews**: After reading a book, encourage your child to write a book review. They can share their opinions, favorite parts, and recommend it to others. This activity helps them practice summarizing and expressing their thoughts about what they have read.

- **Creative Writing Prompts:** Provide creative writing prompts that challenge your child's imagination. For example, "Write a story about a talking animal that goes on an adventure" or "Imagine you discovered a hidden treasure in your backyard." This sparks their creativity and allows them to explore different writing styles.

- **Pen Pals:** Find a pen pal for your child, either through school or online platforms. They can exchange letters or emails with their pen pal, sharing stories, interests, and experiences. This activity improves their writing skills and provides an opportunity for meaningful communication.

- **Writing Contests or Challenges**: Encourage your child to participate in writing contests or challenges, either within their school or online. This motivates them to write and provides a platform to showcase their skills.

Focus on grammar and punctuation: Introduce basic grammar rules and punctuation marks to your child gradually. Teach them how to use capital letters, periods, commas, and question marks correctly. Help them understand the importance of proper grammar in conveying their ideas effectively.

Offer constructive feedback: When your child writes or communicates, provide constructive feedback to help them improve. Praise their efforts and highlight areas where they can enhance their writing or communication skills. Encourage them to revise and edit their work.

Engage in creative writing activities: Spark your child's imagination and creativity by engaging them in creative writing activities. Encourage them to write stories, poems, or even simple plays. Celebrate their creativity and provide a supportive environment for their writing endeavors.

Play language games: Incorporate language games into your daily routine. Engage in word puzzles, rhyming games, or charades that promote language development and communication skills. Make learning fun and enjoyable for your child. Here are some fun language games for 6-10-year-old kids:

- **Rhyme Time**: Select a word, and take turns coming up with words that rhyme with it. Encourage your child to be creative and think of as many rhyming words as possible.

- **I Spy with Words:** Instead of using colors or objects, play "I Spy" using words. Choose a word and provide hints about its characteristics or beginning sounds. Your child can guess the word based on the clues.

- **Category Carousel:** Choose a category like animals, fruits, or colors. Take turns naming items within that category, starting with each letter of the alphabet. For example, "A is for apple, B is for banana," and so on.

- **Story Chain**: Begin a story with a few sentences, and then have your child add a few more sentences to continue the story. Take turns building on each other's ideas and see where the story leads.

- **Alphabet Adventures**: Go on an alphabet adventure where you take turns finding objects or words that start with each letter of the alphabet. For example, "A is for apple, B is for ball," and so on.

- **Synonym Seeker:** Select a word and challenge your child to come up with as many synonyms as possible. This game helps expand their vocabulary and encourages them to explore different words with similar meanings.

- **Sentence Scramble:** Create sentence cards with words jumbled up. Your child needs to unscramble the words to form a complete sentence. Start with simple sentences and increase the complexity as they become more comfortable.

- **Story Mad Libs:** Create Mad Libs-style stories by asking your child for specific types of words (e.g., noun, adjective, verb) without revealing the context. Fill in the blanks with their chosen words, and then read the hilarious story aloud.

- **Tongue Twisters:** Challenge your child with tongue twisters and see if they can say them correctly without stumbling over the words. This game helps improve pronunciation and fluency.

Read together and discuss: Reading together is not only beneficial for developing reading skills but also for enhancing communication skills. After reading a book or a story, engage in discussions with your child. Ask them open-ended questions and encourage them to express their thoughts and opinions.

Practical Skills

Teaching your children household chores, DIY tasks, cleaning, and time management is essential. These skills go beyond everyday responsibilities; they are the secret ingredients to raising confident, capable, and independent people. By introducing practical skills at an early age, you equip your children with the tools they need to navigate through life with confidence and competence. Household chores teach them the value of teamwork and responsibility, DIY tasks unlock their creativity and problem-solving abilities, and cleaning cultivates a sense of order and pride in their environment. These skills build character and resilience. Additionally, time management sets the foundation for a balanced and organized life. Let's embark on this exciting journey of practical skills together and empower our little ones for a lifetime of success!

Household Tasks

Imagine a world where our kids confidently take on household chores, demonstrating the capabilities of responsible individuals handling everyday tasks! By involving them in these responsibilities, we're imparting valuable life skills that will remain with them forever. Not only will they learn to share the load, but they'll also develop a strong sense of responsibility and accomplishment. They'll become masters of sorting laundry, transforming the chaos of clothes into a triumph of cleanliness and organization. They'll conquer the bed-making battle by turning messy beds into cozy havens fit for royalty. Here's how you can teach your kids some common household tasks:

Sorting Laundry:

Teaching your kids how to sort laundry is a fun and interactive experience that helps them develop important skills. By involving them in the process, you can turn it into a game and make them aware of the importance of sorting by colors and fabric types. This activity not only prevents color bleeding and damage to clothes but also instills a sense of responsibility in your little ones. Show them how to create separate piles for whites, darks, and delicate items, and engage them in a conversation about each garment's color and fabric. You can even make it more exciting by creating fun labels or signs for each pile. By transforming laundry sorting into a detective mission, you empower your kids to become laundry pros and protect their clothes from potential color disaster.

Making Bed:

Empower your children with the valuable skill of making their bed by providing them with step-by-step instructions. Take the time to demonstrate the process, showing them how to tuck in sheets, fluff pillows, and arrange blankets with precision. Encourage them to take pride in their ability to create a neat and cozy space each morning. By incorporating bed-making into their daily routine, you teach them the importance of organization and responsibility. With your guidance and support, they will soon become masters of bed-making, setting the stage for a more organized and productive day ahead.

Vacuum Cleaning:

Get ready to introduce your little ones to the exciting world of vacuum cleaning! Start by demonstrating the safe and proper use of the vacuum cleaner. Show them how to handle the machine, maneuver it across different surfaces, and reach those tricky corners. Make it an interactive experience by letting them have a turn under your guidance. As you demonstrate, emphasize the importance of regular vacuuming to maintain a clean and hygienic environment. Explain how the vacuum cleaner helps to remove dust, dirt, and allergens from floors and carpets, making the home a healthier place to live. Encourage them to take pride in keeping their surroundings clean and teach them that vacuuming is an essential part of household chores.

Dusting And Cleaning:

Before getting started, provide them with suitable tools like dusters, microfiber cloths, or child-friendly cleaning sprays to make the experience even more exciting. Demonstrate proper dusting techniques by showing them how to wipe surfaces, shelves, and furniture with care and precision. Encourage your children to actively participate in regular cleaning sessions, making it a fun and engaging activity. Let them feel a sense of pride and accomplishment as they take responsibility for keeping their surroundings tidy. By involving them in the cleaning process, you are teaching them valuable life skills while instilling habits of cleanliness and responsibility.

Loading Dishwasher:

Let's dish out some dishwashing wisdom! Show your kids the secret art of loading the dishwasher like a pro. First, teach them the essential step of scraping off those pesky food residues (so the dishwasher doesn't turn into a food fight arena!). Next, guide them in arranging dishes and utensils in their designated compartments, like a jigsaw puzzle of cleanliness. And here's the neat part: explain the superpowers of a dishwasher, like saving water and guaranteeing sparkling, sanitized dishes. It's like having a magical cleaning wizard right in your kitchen! So, gather your little helpers, pass on your dishwashing knowledge, and let the clean and tidy kitchen adventures begin!

Manual Dishwashing:
Show your little ones the step-by-step magic of getting those dishes squeaky clean. Start by filling the sink with warm, bubbly, soapy water, creating a mini foam party for your dishes. Then, guide your kids through the art of scrubbing, making sure every plate, bowl, and utensil gets the VIP treatment. Rinse away the suds under running water, ensuring they're sparkling clean, and finally, let the dishes bask in the glory of air-drying or using a soft towel. Along the way, remind your little helpers about the importance of cleanliness and hygiene, turning dishwashing into a superhero mission against germs.

Basic Gardening:
Introduce your kids to the magical world of gardening by assigning them age-appropriate tasks that will ignite their curiosity and love for nature. Teach them the art of watering plants, showing them the perfect amount of hydration, each plant needs. Unleash their weed-busting skills as they learn to pull out those sneaky intruders, clearing the way for their precious plants to flourish. Show them the wonders of sowing seeds or planting seedlings, allowing them to wit-

ness the awe-inspiring journey from tiny sprout to blooming beauty. And as they care for their garden, encourage them to observe and nurture the growth of their green companions, fostering a deep sense of responsibility and appreciation for the incredible power of nature. Together, you'll create not just a vibrant garden, and grow food, but also a lifelong bond with the natural world. So grab your trowels, don your gardening hats, and let the green-thumb adventures begin!

DIY Jobs:

Teaching kids the art of do-it-yourself (DIY) jobs is like unlocking a treasure chest of fun, learning, and personal growth. Not only do these hands-on activities spark joy and engagement, but they also play a crucial role in their overall development. By empowering children with practical skills, from building birdhouses to crafting their own artwork, they gain a newfound sense of confidence and accomplishment. It's like watching their little hearts soar with pride as they see what they can create with their own hands. Plus, diving into the world of DIY promotes a sense of independence, as they learn to solve problems, think creatively, and take charge of their own projects. Here's how parents can teach their kids the following DIY tasks:

DIY Maintenance jobs around the home

Empowering 6-10-year-olds with simple DIY fix-it jobs around the house is not only a fantastic learning experience but also a wonderful way to build confidence and independence. Engaging them in tasks like assembling a flat pack bookshelf with adult guidance, is much like following LEGO set instructions, and introduces them to basic tools and problem-solving skills. They'll beam with pride as they see their efforts result in a functional piece of furniture. Hanging up a picture or tightening a screw on a squeaky door becomes an exciting adventure, showing them how little actions can make a big difference. Involving them in these fix-it tasks fosters a sense of accomplishment and resourcefulness, setting them up for a lifetime of self-sufficiency and handy skills!

Cooking Basic Dishes:

Get ready for some kitchen adventures with your budding young chefs! It all starts by introducing them to the world of cooking through simple recipes and getting them involved in the magical process. As you embark on this culinary journey, it's essential to teach your child the importance of kitchen safety rules, ensuring they understand how to handle utensils and appliances with care. Show them the ropes of measuring ingredients, teaching them the art of precision and accuracy. Begin with age-appropriate tasks like stirring, mixing, or assembling ingredients, allowing them to feel the joy of being a valuable part of the cooking process. With time and practice, they can gradually progress to more complex dishes under your watchful guidance. It's a recipe for not just delicious meals but also a whole lot of shared memories and skills that will last a lifetime. So, tie those aprons, gather your little chefs, and let the magic of cooking begin!

Eating Healthy:

Teach your child about the importance of nutritious food and involve them in meal planning and preparation. Explain the different food groups, balanced meals, and the benefits of eating a variety of fruits, vegetables, whole grains, and proteins. Take them grocery shopping and let them choose healthy ingredients.

Telling Time:

Start by introducing them to the wonder of analog clocks, those classic time-keepers that bring a touch of nostalgia to our lives. Explain the concepts of hours and minutes, and show them the different parts of a clock, like the hour hand, minute hand, and the numbers on the dial. Demonstrate how to read and interpret the positions of the hands, unravelling the secrets of time. Make it a regular practice by asking your child to tell you the time or setting time-related tasks for them to accomplish. It's like embarking on a thrilling treasure hunt where time is the ultimate prize. With every tick and tock, your child will develop a strong sense of time awareness and sharpen their cognitive skills. Here are some engaging times telling activities for kids:

- **Clock Craft:** Help your child create their own paper clock using cardboard or a paper plate. Label the hours and minutes, and let them decorate it creatively. Practice telling time by setting different scenarios and asking your child to move the clock hands accordingly.

- **Time Bingo:** Create a bingo game with different clocks showing various times. Call out different times, and your child can cover the corresponding clocks on their bingo card. This activity reinforces time recognition and helps them become more familiar with different clock faces.

- **Time Puzzles**: Create puzzle pieces with different clock faces and time representations. Mix them up and challenge your child to match the analog clock with the corresponding digital representation. This activity helps reinforce the connection between analog and digital time.

- **Time Walk:** Take your child on a "time walk" around your house or neighborhood. Set specific time intervals (e.g., every 10 minutes) and ask your child to observe and identify what they see or experience during those intervals. It's a fun way to develop their time awareness and observation skills.

- **Time Math Challenges:** Create math problems related to time, such as calculating the duration of different activities or solving elapsed time puzzles. For example, "If you start watching a 30-minute TV show at 4:15, what time will it end?" This activity combines time-telling skills with mathematical thinking.

- **Time Flashcards:** Make flashcards with different times shown on analog or digital clocks. Show the flashcards to your child, and they can quickly tell you the corresponding time. You can also reverse the activity and ask your child to show you a specific time using a blank clock face.

Reading A Map:

Introduce your child to maps and the basics of navigation. Teach them how to understand symbols, legends, and scales on a map. Start with simple maps of your neighborhood and help them identify landmarks, streets, and directions. Engage in map-based activities or treasure hunts to make it interactive and enjoyable. Here are some fun and educational map-reading activities for kids:

- **Neighborhood Scavenger Hunt**: Create a map of your neighborhood or a nearby park, marking key locations or landmarks. Provide your child with a copy of the map and challenge them to find the hidden treasures or complete specific tasks along the way.

- **Treasure Map Adventure:** Draw a pirate-themed treasure map with clues and X marks the spot. Let your child follow the map to discover the hidden treasure (which could be a small treat or a special surprise) buried in your backyard or indoors.

- **Create a Fantasy Land**: Encourage your child to create their own imaginative map of a make-believe land. They can include mountains, forests, rivers, and even fantasy creatures. Let their creativity flow as they design their dream world on paper.

- **Road Trip Planner**: If you have a family trip coming up, involve your child in planning the route using a road map or a digital map application. Ask them to identify landmarks or interesting places along the way and mark them on the map. This activity helps develop their navigation and research skills.

- **Nature Exploration Map**: Take your child on a nature walk in a nearby park or forest. Together, observe the surroundings and collect natural objects like leaves, rocks, or flowers. Later, sit down and create a map showcasing the different areas and the treasures found during the exploration.

Managing Time:

Teach your child the importance of time management by setting routines and schedules. Help them create a visual timetable or use a planner to organize their activities and responsibilities. Encourage them to prioritize tasks, set goals, and allocate appropriate time for different activities such as homework, playtime, and chores. Here are some engaging time management activities for kids:

- **Daily Schedule Creation**: Help your child create a daily schedule or routine. Use a visual chart or a whiteboard where they can write down different activities and allocate specific time slots for each task. This activity teaches them to plan and manage their time effectively.

- **Time-Tracking Challenge**: Give your child a stopwatch or a timer and challenge them to complete tasks within a set time limit. For example, they can try to tidy up their room in 10 minutes or finish a puzzle within 15 minutes. This activity promotes time awareness and encourages them to work efficiently.

- **Time Estimation Game**: Engage your child in a game where they estimate how long different activities take. For example, ask them to guess how long it will take to brush their teeth or complete a drawing. Afterward, compare their estimates with the actual time it takes. This activity helps them develop a sense of time duration.

- **Countdown Timer Challenge**: Set up a countdown timer for various activities, such as cleaning up toys or completing a homework assignment. Encourage your child to beat the clock and finish the task before the time runs out. This activity enhances their time management and task prioritization skills.

- **Time Block Planning**: Teach your child about time blocking by dividing their day into blocks of time for different activities. They can use colorful blocks or sticky notes to represent each activity. Help them understand the importance of allocating dedicated time for various tasks like homework, playtime, reading, and chores.

- **Calendar Marking:** Provide your child with a calendar where they can mark important events, deadlines, or activities. This helps them visualize upcoming events and manage their time accordingly. They can also learn to prioritize tasks by marking them with different symbols or colors.

Caring For Pets:

Teach your child about pet care responsibilities, including feeding, grooming, and cleaning up after pets. Show them how to handle pets gently and responsibly. Assign age-appropriate tasks like filling water bowls, brushing fur, or assisting in walking the pet. Instil empathy and the importance of providing a loving and safe environment for animals.

During this process make sure to provide clear instructions, supervise your child initially, and gradually give them more independence as they become proficient in each task. Celebrate their accomplishments and offer encouragement throughout the learning process. By teaching these DIY tasks, you're equipping your child with essential life skills that will serve them well as they grow and navigate the world with confidence.

MANAGING EMOTIONS AND PROBLEM-SOLVING

You know those moments when your little one goes from laughter to tears in a split second? Yeah, we've all been there. By teaching them about managing emotions, we're equipping them with valuable skills to handle those ups and downs with grace (or at least a little less chaos). They'll learn to express their feelings in healthy ways, communicate better, and build positive relationships with others. Plus, who doesn't want a household that feels like a calm and happy oasis? Together, we'll guide our little ones to manage their emotions skillfully and approach problem-solving like experts, raising a generation of emotionally intelligent individuals ready to take on the world with a twinkle in their eyes and a whole lot of giggles..

Recognizing And Expressing Emotions

Teaching our kids to recognize and express emotions is like providing them with a valuable key to understanding themselves and the world around them. It's an essential life skill that forms the foundation of emotional intelligence. By helping them identify and label their emotions, we empower them to navigate their inner world with clarity and self-awareness. When our kids can effectively express their emotions, they become better equipped to communicate their needs, wants, and boundaries. As a result, they develop stronger relationships, as their friends and family can understand how they're feeling and offer support. Additionally, expressing emotions in a healthy way reduces stress and promotes emotional well-being. It's akin to unlocking a treasure chest of resilience and emotional balance..

So, how can we help our little ones on this emotional journey? Here are some techniques you can use:

Create an Emotion-Friendly Environment: Foster an open and accepting atmosphere where all emotions are welcomed and validated. Let your kids know it's okay to feel sad, angry, or happy. Celebrate the array of emotions!

Empathy and Active Listening: Encourage empathy by listening attentively to your child's emotions. Reflect on what you hear, show understanding, and let them know you're there for them.

Name the Emotion: Help your child identify and label their emotions. Use words like "I see you're feeling frustrated" or "It sounds like you're really excited!" This helps them develop a vocabulary for expressing their feelings.

Artistic Expression: Engage in creative activities like drawing, painting, or writing to encourage emotional expression. Let their imaginations run wild as they create masterpieces that capture their emotions.

Emotion Charades: Play a fun game of emotion charades, where your child acts out different emotions and others guess what they're feeling. This helps them understand body language and facial expressions.

Strategies For Problem-Solving and Decision-Making

Skills to solve problems at hand and making conscious well-informed decisions are crucial for children as they foster independence, critical thinking, and resilience. These skills empower children to tackle challenges on their own, think critically, and persevere in the face of setbacks. By developing problem-solving skills, children become more self-reliant and confident in their abilities, while also enhancing their analytical and logical reasoning abilities. They learn to plan, set goals, and break down complex problems into manageable parts. Additionally, problem-solving and decision-making teach children responsibility and accountability for their choices, as well as the importance of considering consequences.

These skills promote collaboration, communication, and adaptability. Children learn to work effectively in teams, listen to different perspectives, and communicate their ideas. Through problem-solving and decision-making, children develop a positive attitude toward overcoming obstacles and understand that setbacks are a natural part of life, and that there is an opportunity to learn from the experience. By fostering these skills, parents help their children navigate challenges, make informed choices, and build the confidence and resilience needed for future success in various aspects of life. Here are some strategies for your kids to enhance their problem-solving and decision-making skills:

Critical Thinking: Foster your child's critical thinking skills by encouraging them to question and analyze situations. Teach them to recognize when something lacks logical reasoning and instill in them the value of seeking the truth. Engage in discussions about the potential consequences of being deceived by others and introduce them to reliable sources for finding credible information.

Activities to instigate critical thinking in kids:

- **Mystery Solving**: Present your child with riddles or puzzles that require them to think critically and use logical reasoning to solve the mystery.

- **Fact-Checking**: Choose a topic of interest and together, research different sources to determine which ones are trustworthy and reliable. Teach your child how to evaluate information and make informed judgments.

- **Socratic Questioning**: Engage your child in conversations where you ask thought-provoking questions to encourage them to think deeply and express their ideas and reasoning.

- **Problem Scenarios**: Create hypothetical scenarios where your child must analyze the situation and propose solutions. Encourage them to consider different perspectives and weigh the pros and cons of each option.

- **Science Experiments**: Conduct simple science experiments that require observation, prediction, and logical thinking. Encourage your child to question the results and think critically about the underlying principles.

- **Brainstorming Sessions**: Sit down with your child and brainstorm creative solutions to real-world problems or challenges they may encounter. Encourage them to think outside the box and explore multiple possibilities.

Learning from Mistakes: Instill in your child the understanding that making mistakes is a normal and valuable part of the learning and growth process. Guide them in reflecting on their mistakes, exploring the reasons behind them, and brainstorming strategies to prevent similar errors in the future. Highlight the significance of learning from experience and the resilience needed to bounce back from setbacks. Learn to view failure as an opportunity to learn and for personal growth.

Goal Setting: Spark your child's understanding of the impact of goal setting. Guide them in recognizing their aspirations and assist them in breaking those goals into smaller, achievable tasks. Inspire them to maintain their focus, demonstrate perseverance, and celebrate each milestone they reach. By doing so, you will nurture their ability to work towards goals with determination and dedication.

Activities to encourage goal setting in children:

- **Vision Board Creation**: Help your child create a visual representation of their goals by making a vision board. They can cut out pictures or words from magazines that represent their aspirations and display them in a creative collage.

- **Goal Journaling**: Encourage your child to keep a journal where they can write down their goals, along with the specific steps they plan to take to achieve them. Encourage regular reflection and updates on their progress.

- **Personal Goal-Setting Sessions**: Set aside dedicated time to have one-on-one conversations with your child about their goals. Help them articulate what they want to accomplish and discuss strategies for breaking down their goals into actionable steps.

- **Progress Celebrations**: Create a system where you and your child can celebrate their progress along the way. This can involve small rewards, special activities, or simply acknowledging their efforts and achievements.

- **Role-Playing Scenarios**: Engage in role-playing activities where your child can imagine achieving their goals. Encourage them to think about the challenges they might face and brainstorm strategies to overcome them.

- **Decision-Making**: Guide your child through the process of decision-making. Encourage them to consider different options, weigh the pros and cons, and think about the potential consequences of their choices. Teach them to trust their instincts and make decisions based on their values and what feels right to them.

- **Problem-Solving Activities**: Engage your child in interactive problem-solving activities. Puzzles, riddles, scavenger hunts, and brain teasers are all great ways to exercise their problem-solving muscles. These activities will challenge their critical thinking, encourage creativity, and sharpen their decision-making skills in a fun and engaging manner.

Building Resilience and Coping Skills

By instilling resilience and coping skills in children, we equip them with valuable tools that can positively impact their mental health and overall development. Resilience helps children develop a sense of inner strength, optimism, and determination. It allows them to face obstacles with a more positive and proactive mindset, enabling them to persevere and find solutions even when faced with adversity. Coping skills, on the other hand, provide children with a repertoire of strategies to manage stress, regulate their emotions, and solve problems effectively. These skills enable children to identify their feelings, express themselves appropriately, seek support when needed, and make healthy choices in challenging situations. By developing coping skills, children become better equipped to handle everyday stressors, conflicts, and setbacks, which ultimately promotes their well-being and overall resilience. Here are some strategies to help children develop resilience and coping skills:

Encourage a Growth Mindset: Guide your children to embrace setbacks as chances for growth and learning. Foster their understanding that mistakes and failures are normal and provide valuable opportunities for improvement and development through effort and perseverance. Some activities to promote a growth mindset in children include:

- **Praise Effort**: Encourage and acknowledge children's efforts rather than solely focusing on their achievements. Highlight the process they went through and the strategies they used to overcome challenges.

- **Set Goal-Oriented Tasks:** Help children set realistic goals and break them down into manageable steps. Support them in tracking their progress, celebrating milestones, and adjusting their approach when necessary.

- **Encourage Reflection**: Create a routine for children to reflect on their experiences, including both successes and setbacks. Prompt them to identify lessons learned, areas for improvement, and alternative strategies they can try next time.

- **Introduce Inspirational Role Models**: Share stories of individuals who have faced challenges and demonstrated a growth mindset. Discuss how these role models embraced setbacks and used them as opportunities for growth and achievement.

- **Emphasize the Power of "Yet"**: Encourage children to add the word "yet" to their vocabulary when faced with something they haven't mastered. For instance, instead of saying "I can't do it," they can say "I can't do it yet, but I will keep trying and improving."

- **Teach Positive Self-Talk:** Help children recognize and replace negative self-talk with positive and affirming statements. Encourage them to be kind to themselves and believe in their ability to learn and grow.

- **Engage in Problem-Solving Activities**: Provide children with puzzles, brainteasers, and challenging tasks that require them to think creatively and persistently. Encourage them to approach these activities with a growth mindset, focusing on the process rather than the outcome.

Foster Emotional Awareness: Help children recognize and understand their emotions. Encourage them to express their feelings in a healthy and constructive way, whether through talking, writing, drawing, or engaging in activities that promote emotional expression.

Teach Problem-Solving Skills: Support children in their problem-solving journey by guiding them to explore various solutions, assess potential outcomes, and make informed decisions. Encouraging the development of problem-solving skills empowers children to approach challenges with confidence and resilience.

- **Brainstorming Sessions:** Engage children in brainstorming sessions where they can freely generate ideas to solve a specific problem. Encourage them to think creatively and consider different perspectives or approaches.

- **Puzzle Solving**: Provide puzzles or riddles that require logical thinking and problem-solving. Encourage children to tackle them independently or collaborate with others to find solutions.

- **Scavenger Hunts:** Organize scavenger hunts with clues and challenges that require problem-solving skills. Children will need to think critically, analyze information, and strategize to progress through the hunt.

- **Building and Construction**: Offer building blocks, construction sets, or craft materials that allow children to create and solve problems. Encourage them to design and build structures, solve design challenges, or fix and improve their creations.

- **Role-Playing Games**: Engage children in role-playing games where they encounter problems or conflicts that require creative solutions. This helps them practice critical thinking, decision-making, and problem-solving in a fun and imaginative way.

- **Real-Life Scenarios**: Present children with age-appropriate real-life situations or dilemmas and encourage them to analyze the problem, consider different options, and propose solutions. Discuss the potential consequences of each approach to develop their decision-making skills.

- **Journaling**: Encourage children to keep a problem-solving journal where they can record and reflect on challenges they encounter and the strategies they use to solve them. This helps them build problem-solving skills and provides an opportunity for self-reflection.

Promote Healthy Relationships: Teach children the importance of seeking support from family, friends, and trusted adults. Encourage them to communicate their needs, ask for help when necessary, and develop positive relationships that provide a strong support system.

Build Resilience through Play: Involve children in resilience-building activities that foster problem-solving, adaptability, and perseverance through role-playing, imaginative play, and outdoor adventures. These interactive experiences provide a fun and engaging platform for children to develop their resilience skills. Some activities to promote resilience in children are:

- **Role-Playing:** Encourage children to act out different scenarios where they encounter challenges or setbacks. Guide them to brainstorm and demonstrate resilient responses, finding creative solutions and bouncing back from adversity.

- **Imaginative Play**: Provide open-ended toys and materials that allow children to create their own stories and worlds. Through imaginative play, they can navigate obstacles, handle unexpected situations, and develop resilience in a make-believe setting.

- **Outdoor Adventures**: Engage children in nature-based activities such as hiking, camping, or exploring new environments. These experiences expose them to unfamiliar situations and encourage problem-solving in a different context. This builds their adaptability and resilience to changing circumstances.

- **Team Building Exercises:** Arrange activities that require teamwork and cooperation, such as building projects or group games. Encourage children to communicate, collaborate, and problem-solve together, fostering resilience through collective efforts.

- **Reflection and Discussion**: After engaging in challenging activities or facing setbacks, give your children a safe space so that they can think back on their experiences without the fear of being judged or reprimanded. Engage in open and supportive discussions where they can share their emotions, identify lessons learned, and develop strategies for overcoming future obstacles.

- **Storytelling and Books:** Read books or share stories that highlight resilient characters and their journeys. Discuss the challenges the characters face and how they demonstrate resilience. Encourage children to relate these stories to their own lives and explore ways to apply resilience in their everyday situations.

Foster a Positive Outlook: Encourage children to focus on the positive aspects of situations and find gratitude in their lives. Help them reframe challenges as opportunities and celebrate their achievements, no matter how small. Teach children positive self-talk by introducing affirmations and empowering statements. Encourage them to repeat affirmations that promote resilience, such as "I am capable of overcoming challenges" or "I can learn from my mistakes and grow stronger."

Encourage Self-Care: Teach children the importance of taking care of their physical and emotional well-being. Encourage healthy habits such as regular exercise, sufficient sleep, balanced nutrition, and engaging in activities they enjoy.

Be a Role Model: Model resilience and coping skills yourself. Show your child how you handle challenges, setbacks, and stress in a positive and adaptive way. Children often learn best by observing the behaviors of their parents and caregivers.

Facing Fears and Building Confidence

By teaching our kids to confront their fears, we empower them to face challenges head-on. Whether it's a fear of spiders, public speaking, or trying a new sport, guiding them through these fears enhances their resilience and self-belief. It's like equipping them with the secret sauce to navigate life's obstacles with courage and determination. They'll come to understand that fear is merely a temporary roadblock, not dead-end. Picture your child standing tall, shoulders back, and radiating self-assurance. Witnessing their inner glow shine like a little superstar. By nurturing their confidence, we set the stage for their success in all aspects of life. They'll develop a positive self-image, belief in their abilities, and the resilience to bounce back from setbacks. Whether acing a school presentation or making new friends, confidence will be their trusted ally. So, let's shower them with words of encouragement, celebrate their achievements (big or small), and watch their confidence soar to new heights!

Addressing Common Fears and Anxieties

Addressing common fears and anxieties in children is an essential aspect of nurturing their emotional well-being. Childhood is a time of growth, exploration, and new experiences, which can sometimes trigger fears and anxieties. By addressing these emotions, parents and caregivers can provide a supportive and comforting environment that allows children to develop resilience and cope with their fears in a healthy way. Here are some strategies to help children overcome their fears and anxieties:

Create a Safe and Supportive Environment: Foster an atmosphere of trust and open communication. Let your child know that they can talk to you about their fears and anxieties without judgment or criticism. Offer reassurance and comfort when they are feeling scared or anxious.

Validate Their Feelings: Acknowledge and validate your child's emotions. Let them know that it is normal to feel afraid or anxious at times. Help them understand that their feelings are valid and that they are not alone in experiencing these emotions.

Provide Information and Education: Help your child gain a better understanding of their fears or anxieties. Provide age-appropriate information about what they are afraid of or anxious about. Knowledge can often alleviate fears and help children feel more in control of the situation.

Encourage Expression: Encourage your child to express their fears and anxieties through conversation, writing, drawing, or other creative outlets. This allows them to externalize their emotions and gain a sense of release.

Go for Relaxation Techniques: Some effective techniques like deep breathing exercises, visualization, or progressive muscle relaxation are effective when it comes to calming the mind down. These techniques can help calm your child's mind and body during moments of fear or anxiety. Tell them to take 3 deep breaths and count as they breath when they feel angry or frustrated. This will help them learn how to stay calm in tense situations.

Gradual Exposure: Gradually expose your child to the things that trigger their fears or anxieties. Start with small steps and gradually increase the exposure over time. Encourage and support them through each step, providing reassurance and praise for their bravery.

Role Play: Use role-playing to help your child practice coping strategies and problem-solving skills. Pretend to be in situations that cause fear or anxiety and guide your child through how they can respond in a confident and empowered manner.

Encouraging Bravery and Trying New Things

By instilling a sense of bravery, children learn to overcome their fears and take on challenges with confidence. They develop resilience, as they understand that setbacks and failures are part of the learning process. Encouraging children to try new things also nurtures their curiosity and sparks their creativity, as they explore different activities, hobbies, and interests. Here are some strategies to foster bravery and a sense of adventure in children:

Create a Supportive Environment: Creating a safe and supportive environment for children is paramount in fostering their growth and encouraging them to step out of their comfort zone. When children feel safe and supported, they are more likely to take risks, explore new opportunities, and develop their skills and abilities.

One crucial aspect of providing a safe environment is emphasizing that making mistakes is a natural part of learning and growth. By assuring children that mistakes are valuable learning experiences and not something to be feared or ashamed of, they feel more confident in taking on challenges. Letting them know that you believe in their abilities and that you are there to support them unconditionally builds their self-esteem and encourages them to embrace new experiences.

Start Small and Build Confidence: Starting with small challenges and gradually increasing the level of difficulty is a proven method to help children develop bravery and a willingness to try new things. By introducing age-appropriate tasks that push their boundaries, children can experience a sense of accomplishment as they overcome each challenge.

The key is to find a balance between providing challenges that are engaging and stimulating, but not too overwhelming. Beginning with manageable tasks allows children to build confidence and develop a positive mindset towards taking on new experiences. As they successfully conquer these smaller challenges, their belief in their abilities grows, and they become more willing to step outside their comfort zone.

Praise Effort and Resilience:

Focus on your child's effort and resilience rather than just the outcome. Celebrate their willingness to try, their perseverance, and their ability to learn from both successes and failures. This reinforces the value of taking risks and developing a growth mindset.

Encourage Exploration and Curiosity:

Ignite your child's curiosity by providing them with diverse experiences and opportunities to explore. Encourage them to delve into their interests, experiment with various hobbies, and uncover hidden talents. By exposing them to a range of activities, you help broaden their horizons and instill a sense of confidence when it comes to embracing new experiences. Here are some activities to foster resilience and curiosity in children:

- **"Discovery Jar"**: Create a jar filled with small slips of paper, each containing a different activity or adventure. Encourage your child to randomly select a slip and embark on the corresponding activity. This could include visiting a museum, trying a new sport, or learning a musical instrument. This activity encourages exploration and opens new avenues for your child's interests and talents.

- **"Passion Project"**: Help your child identify a topic or subject they are passionate about. Guide them in researching and delving deeper into the subject, allowing them to explore different aspects and develop their knowledge. This activity fosters resilience as it requires dedication, perseverance, and the ability to overcome obstacles while pursuing their passion.

- **"Try-It Tuesdays"**: Dedicate one day of the week to trying something new. Encourage your child to engage in activities they have never attempted before, such as cooking a new recipe, practicing a new dance routine, or attempting a science experiment. This activity promotes resilience by teaching children to embrace challenges and adapt to new situations.

Provide a Supportive Network: Surround your child with supportive and encouraging individuals who inspire and motivate them to be brave. This can include family members, friends, mentors, or participation in group activities where they can learn from and support one another.

Normalize Failure as a Learning Opportunity: Teach your child that failure is a natural part of life and an opportunity for growth. Help them understand that setbacks are not permanent and that they can learn valuable lessons from their experiences.

Celebrate Achievements: Celebrate and acknowledge your child's bravery and achievements. Whether big or small, recognizing their efforts boosts their self-esteem and motivates them to continue trying new things.

Developing Self-Confidence and Self-Esteem

A confident child is a happy child who communicates effectively with others and stands up for themselves in challenging situations. This confidence is nurtured by the support provided by their parents. Creating a safe and nurturing environment through unconditional love and encouragement allows children to flourish. Believing in their abilities and strengths is crucial, as it instills a sense of worth and validates their uniqueness. Celebrating their achievements, no matter how small, fosters a positive sense of accomplishment and encourages them to take pride in their efforts. Here are some strategies to further support your child's self-confidence and self-esteem:

Provide Unconditional Love and Support: Unconditional love and acceptance are fundamental for a child's self-esteem. Show your child that you love them for who they are, regardless of their achievements or failures. Offer support and encouragement, emphasizing that your love is not based on their performance.

Focus on Strengths and Positive Qualities: Recognize and celebrate your child's strengths and positive qualities. Encourage them to explore their interests and talents. Help them identify their unique abilities and accomplishments, which boosts their self-confidence.

Encourage Independence and Decision-Making: Give your child opportunities to make decisions and take responsibility for their actions. This helps build their confidence in their ability to navigate the world. Offer guidance and support while allowing them to learn from their choices. Here are some activities that can help foster these skills:

- **Age-appropriate responsibilities**: Assign your child age-appropriate tasks and responsibilities around the house. This can include setting the table, organizing their belongings, or helping with simple household chores. Encourage them to take ownership of these tasks and complete them independently.

- **Problem-solving challenges**: Present your child with problem-solving challenges or puzzles that require them to think critically and come up with solutions. This can be in the form of riddles, brain teasers, or even simple DIY projects. Support them by asking guiding questions to help them think through the problem.

- **Decision-making games**: Engage your child in decision-making games where they must make choices and consider the consequences. This can be as simple as asking them to choose what activity to do or what book to read. Encourage them to weigh the pros and cons and make informed decisions.

- **Planning and organizing:** Involve your child in planning and organizing activities, such as planning a family outing or organizing their school materials. This helps them develop skills in setting goals, prioritizing tasks, and managing their time effectively.

- **Role-playing scenarios**: Create role-playing scenarios where your child can practice making decisions and dealing with different situations. This can include pretend play as a store owner, doctor, or problem-solving detective. Encourage them to think critically, consider different perspectives, and make choices accordingly.

- **Real-life experiences**: Provide opportunities for your child to experience real-life decision-making situations. This can involve letting them choose their own outfit, decide on extracurricular activities, or plan a small event. Offer guidance and support but allow them to have a sense of autonomy and learn from their choices.

Provide Constructive Feedback: Offer constructive feedback that focuses on effort, improvement, and specific actions. Highlight their achievements and point out areas where they can grow and develop. This helps them see setbacks as learning opportunities rather than personal failures.

Encourage Goal Setting and Achievement: Help your child set realistic goals and support them in working towards those goals. Break bigger goals into smaller, achievable steps, and celebrate milestones along the way. This instills a sense of accomplishment and reinforces their belief in their abilities.

Teach Problem-Solving and Resilience: Help your child develop problem-solving skills and resilience by encouraging them to find solutions to challenges on their own. Guide them in overcoming obstacles and teach them to bounce back from setbacks. This fosters confidence in their ability to handle difficult situations.

Foster Positive Relationships: Surround your child with positive and supportive relationships. Encourage friendships with peers who uplift and respect them. Provide opportunities for them to engage in social activities where they can build relationships and develop interpersonal skills.

Model Positive Self-Talk and Confidence: Be mindful of your own self-talk and how you express confidence. Model positive self-esteem and speak positively about yourself and others. Children learn from observing their parents, so by demonstrating self-confidence, you inspire them to do the same.

Navigating Social Skills and Relationships

Teaching our kids how to navigate social skills and relationships lays the foundation for success in the wild and wonderful world of human interaction. They'll embrace the art of communication, empathy, and cooperation, transforming into adept social individuals. These skills go beyond making friends and fitting in; they open doors to meaningful connections, teamwork, and resolving conflicts with finesse.

Nurturing their social skills gifts our kids with the ability to build strong relationships that can last a lifetime. They'll understand the value of active listening, taking turns, and respecting others' thoughts and feelings. Picture them engaging in conversations effortlessly, confidently sharing their ideas, and making a positive impact on those around them. It's like observing little social butterflies spreading their wings and brightening everyone's day!

Understanding The Importance of Kindness and Empathy

Teaching your children, the importance of kindness and empathy is essential for fostering positive relationships, building a compassionate society, and nurturing their own emotional well-being. By understanding and practicing kindness, children learn to treat others with respect, empathy, and compassion. They develop the ability to recognize and empathize with the feelings and needs of others, promoting inclusivity and understanding. Kindness also cultivates a sense of gratitude and appreciation for the people and world around them. Moreover, when children experience acts of kindness and witness their positive impact, they develop a strong sense of self-worth and fulfillment, leading to enhanced social connections and overall happiness.

Lead by Example: Model kindness and empathy in your own behavior. Show compassion and understanding towards others, including family members, friends, and even strangers. Children learn by observing, so your actions have a powerful impact on their understanding of kindness and empathy.

Teach Perspective-Taking: Help your child develop the ability to see situations from other people's perspectives. Encourage them to imagine how someone else might be feeling or experiencing a situation. This helps cultivate empathy and a deeper understanding of others.

Some interesting activities to teach perspective-taking are:

- "**Walk in Their Shoes**": Create a "Walk in Their Shoes" activity where children can choose a family member, friend, or fictional character and imagine what it would be like to be in their position. They can write or draw about their experiences, sharing insights into the challenges and emotions that person may face.

- **Cultural Experiences:** Expose children to different cultures and traditions through activities like trying diverse cuisines, attending cultural festivals, or exploring art and music from various parts of the world. This helps broaden their understanding of different perspectives and fosters appreciation for diversity.

- **Problem-Solving Scenarios**: Present children with hypothetical problem-solving scenarios where they must consider multiple perspectives. Have them think critically and of solutions that consider the needs and feelings of others involved.

- **Interview and Share**: Ask your children to interview family members or friends about their experiences, interests, and opinions. They can then share what they've learned with others, promoting understanding and empathy.

Promote Open Communication: Create an open and safe space for your child to express their feelings and thoughts. Encourage them to talk about their own emotions and experiences. Listen attentively and validate their feelings, showing them that their emotions are important and worthy of empathy.

Teach Compassionate Communication: Teach your child to communicate in a kind and respectful manner. Encourage them to use words that show understanding and empathy, such as "How can I help?" or "I understand how you feel." Model this type of communication in your own interactions with them and others.

Encourage Acts of Kindness: Promote acts of kindness in your child's daily life. Encourage them to help others, whether it's a family member, friend, or someone in the community. Engage in random acts of kindness together, such as writing thank-you notes or donating to a charitable cause.

Here are some creative ideas to encourage kindness in your kids:

- **Kindness Coupons**: Have children create their own kindness coupons that offer acts of kindness to family members, such as cooking a meal, cleaning their room, or giving them a hug. Encourage them to use these coupons throughout the week.

- **Acts of Service**: Involve children in acts of service within the community, such as cleaning up a park, visiting a nursing home, or assisting in a neighborhood clean-up. These activities promote kindness and empathy towards others.

- **Kindness Challenge:** Set up a kindness challenge where children must complete a certain number of kind acts within a specific timeframe. Provide them with a list of ideas or let them come up with their own acts of kindness.

- **Appreciation Cards**: Encourage children to make handmade appreciation cards for teachers, family members, or friends. These cards can express gratitude and kindness towards the recipient.

Expose Them to Different Perspectives: Expose your child to diverse experiences, cultures, and perspectives. Read books together that explore different cultures and discuss the importance of understanding and respecting differences. This helps broaden their worldview and nurtures empathy towards others.

Encourage Problem-Solving with Kindness: Teach your child to resolve conflicts and solve problems in a kind and empathetic manner. Encourage them to consider other people's feelings and perspectives when finding solutions. Help them understand that kindness can be a powerful tool in resolving conflicts and building positive relationships.

Practice Gratitude: Cultivate a sense of gratitude in your child by regularly expressing gratitude for the kindness of others and the positive aspects of their own lives. Encourage them to acknowledge and appreciate the efforts and kindness they receive from others.

Developing Effective Communication Skills

As a parent you can play a significant role in helping your children develop effective communication skills. Be an active listener by giving them your full attention and showing genuine interest in what they have to say. Create a safe and supportive environment where they feel comfortable expressing their thoughts and feelings. Model clear communication and teach them about non-verbal cues. Practice empathy and teach conflict resolution skills. Encourage public speaking opportunities and promote reading and writing activities. Provide constructive feedback and engage in role-playing scenarios to develop their communication skills further. By implementing these strategies, parents can nurture their child's communication abilities, helping them become confident and effective communicators. Here are some practical techniques that you can try with your kids:

- **Show and Tell:** Organize a regular "Show and Tell" session where children can bring an item or talk about a topic of interest. This activity promotes effective communication by giving them a platform to express themselves, share their experiences, and engage in discussions.

- **Discussion Circles**: Create a safe and inclusive space for children to participate in group discussions. Choose relevant topics and encourage active listening, turn-taking, and respectful communication. This activity helps them develop their speaking and listening skills while learning to express their opinions and consider different perspectives.

- **Debates or Mock Trials:** Organize friendly debates or mock trials where children can argue different sides of an issue. This activity promotes critical thinking, persuasive speaking, and the ability to present well-structured arguments.

- **Interview Skills:** Help children develop interview skills by role-playing as interviewers and interviewees. They can practice asking and answering questions effectively, maintaining eye contact, and using appropriate body language.

- **Collaborative Projects**: Engage children in group projects that require them to work together and communicate effectively. This could be creating a presentation, organizing an event, or solving a problem as a team. Encourage them to listen to each other, share ideas, and communicate clearly to achieve their common goal.

- **Story Discussions**: After reading a book or watching a movie, facilitate discussions where children can share their thoughts, analyze characters' motivations, and interpret the story's themes. This activity helps them improve their comprehension skills and express their ideas with clarity.

- **Journaling**: Encourage children to keep a journal where they can write about their thoughts, feelings, and experiences. This practice helps them develop written communication skills and self-expression.

- **Public Speaking Opportunities**: Provide opportunities for children to speak in front of others, such as presenting in class, participating in school events, or joining a public speaking club. This helps build confidence and effective communication skills.

- **Active Listening Exercises**: Engage children in activities that promote active listening, such as listening to and summarizing a story or following instructions for a task. This helps them develop their listening skills, which are essential for effective communication.

Resolving Conflicts and Making Friends

Conflict resolution skills are essential for children to learn how to handle disagreements and disputes in a healthy and constructive way. Parents can teach their kids effective communication strategies, such as active listening, expressing emotions calmly, and finding common ground. By role-playing different conflict scenarios and offering guidance, parents can empower their children with the skills and confidence to address conflicts assertively and peacefully. Here are some strategies to support your child in conflict resolution:

Teach Conflict Resolution Skills: Teach your child effective conflict resolution strategies such as active listening, expressing emotions calmly, and finding mutually agreeable solutions. Encourage them to communicate openly, assertively, and respectfully when faced with conflicts.

Encourage Empathy and Perspective-Taking: Help your child understand the perspectives and feelings of others involved in a conflict. Encourage them to see the situation from different angles and consider how their actions may have impacted others. This helps foster empathy and promotes understanding.

Model Healthy Conflict Resolution: Demonstrate empathy and understanding towards others' perspectives and encourage your child to do the same. Teach them the importance of finding common ground, compromising when necessary, and working towards win-win solutions. If you model such behavior in front of them the mirror neurons in their brain will likely pick that up

Dealing With Bullies:

Helping children develop the skills to deal with bullies is incredibly important for their well-being and growth. By teaching them effective strategies, we empower them to stand up for themselves and others when faced with bullying situations. They learn to assert their boundaries, communicate confidently, and seek support from trusted adults. It's all about giving them the tools and confidence to handle these challenges with resilience and strength. By understanding how to address bullying, children can create a positive and supportive environment where kindness and respect thrive.

Promote Open Communication: Create a safe and non-judgmental space for your child to talk about their experiences with bullying. Encourage them to share their feelings and concerns. Be an active listener and validate their emotions, reassuring them that they are not alone and you are there to support them.

Teach Assertiveness: Teach your child assertiveness skills to confidently respond to bullies. Help them practice assertive body language, strong and clear voice, and the ability to express their feelings and set boundaries. Encourage them to seek help from trusted adults when needed.

Foster Resilience and Self-Confidence: Help your child build resilience and self-esteem through positive reinforcement and highlighting their strengths. Encourage them to engage in activities they enjoy and excel in, which can boost their confidence and make them less vulnerable to bullying.

Making Friends:

Good friendships provide a sense of belonging, support, and companionship. When children learn the skills needed to make and maintain healthy friendships, they cultivate qualities like empathy, kindness, and effective communication. By understanding the importance of mutual respect, active listening, and compromise, children can navigate conflicts and build strong, meaningful connections with others. Having good friends enhances their self-esteem, promotes positive social interactions, and fosters a sense of belonging.

Teach Social Skills: Help your child develop social skills such as active listening, starting conversations, sharing, taking turns, and showing empathy. Role-play social situations with them to practice these skills in a safe and supportive environment.

Encourage Inclusion and Kindness: Teach your child the importance of inclusion and kindness. Encourage them to reach out to others, invite them to join activities, and be inclusive in their interactions. Emphasize the value of empathy and treating others with respect.

Provide Opportunities for Socialization: Arrange playdates, enroll your child in group activities or clubs, and encourage them to participate in social events where they can meet and interact with peers. These experiences provide opportunities for them to develop friendships and practice their social skills.

Be a Supportive Coach: Offer guidance and support to your child in navigating social situations. Help them understand that making friends takes time, and it's okay to experience setbacks. Provide advice on initiating conversations, listening actively, and maintaining positive relationships.

Conclusion

As we come to the end of this incredible journey through the pages of "Empowering Your Under 10: The Essential Life Skills Handbook," we celebrate the transformative power of equipping our children with the tools they need to thrive. From the tender age of 2-3 years old, we foster independence, teach safety, and nurture emotional expression. As they blossom into the ages of 4-5, we cultivate practical life skills, embrace safety awareness, and unlock the wonders of learning and exploration. And while guiding our 6-10-year-olds, we witness the evolution of remarkable young souls.

In these pivotal years, we nurture effective communication, problem-solving prowess, and self-confidence that will serve as their unwavering compass in life's tumultuous sea.

This Handbook is a trusted ally and a treasure trove brimming with nuggets of information that enable you to equip your child to tackle the ups and downs of growing up. From mastering time-telling to honing social skills, this book serves as a training manual, offering a diverse range of techniques to try, so you can discover what works best for your unique child.

Infused with an element of fun, it demonstrates how to become the ultimate sidekicks in guiding kids toward their full potential.

As we conclude, let us embrace the understanding that all kids are different individuals, and what works for one child may not resonate with another. But armed with a collection of techniques and strategies from this Handbook, we can help our children as best we can, nurturing their individuality and celebrating their strengths.

Life's journey is not without its hurdles, but with essential life skills in their arsenal, our children will find their way through the maze of uncertainties, discovering the beauty of resilience and self-love.

May the lessons from this Handbook continue to resonate through the years, reminding us that our role in empowering these young souls is a gift that extends far beyond the pages of any book. With unwavering love and guidance, we lay the foundation for a brighter future, one where these under-10s bloom into compassionate, confident, and empathetic beings.

So, dear parents, caregivers, and mentors, let us continue this voyage together, hand in hand, as we empower our under-10s to embrace life's challenges with wisdom, courage, and an unwavering belief in their limitless potential. For they are the heroes of tomorrow, and we, their steadfast allies, are honored to play a part in their incredible journey.

REFERENCES

"Frontiers | Age-Specific Life Skills Education in School: A Systematic Review." Frontiers, .

13 Fun Ways to Develop Motor Skills in Young Children. (n.d.). Rasmussen University.

Cardon, T. A. (2004). *Let's Talk Emotions: Helping Children with Social Cognitive Deficits, Including AS, HFA, and NVLD, Learn to Understand and Express Empathy and Emotions.* AAPC Publishing.

Caton, G. (1999). What's the difference between fine motor and gross motor skills? *BabyCentre UK*.

Duncan, A. (2022). 11 Life Skills You Should Teach Your Kids. Verywell Family.

Gonzalez, S. L., Alvarez, V. A., & Nelson, E. L. (2019). Do Gross and Fine Motor Skills Differentially Contribute to Language Outcomes? A Systematic Review. *Frontiers in Psychology, 10*.

Help Your Child Build Fine Motor Skills. (n.d.). NAEYC.

Ians. (2021, December 22). Five important life skills you should teach your kids. The Economic Times.

Kim. (2021). How To Teach Your Child to Call 911 in the Cell Phone Age. *Team Cartwright*.

Lewis, R. (2020, July 29). *What Are Gross Motor Skills?* Healthline.

Mauro, T. (2022). Fine and Gross Motor Skills in Children. Verywell Family.

Parents Editors. (2023). Developing Fine Motor Skills in Preschoolers. *Parents*.

Patel, M. (2023). Ways You Can Introduce Plants and Animals to Your Child. *iON Future*.

Perez, S. T. (2022). How to Express Emotions for Kids: Lessons and Activities to Build Self-Awareness. Independently Published.

Prajapati, Ravindra & Sharma, Bosky & Sharma, Dharmendra. (2016). Significance Of Life Skills Education. Contemporary Issues in Education Research (CIER). 10. 1. 10.19030/cier.v10i1.9875.

State, C. F. M. F. R. a. P. (2020, June 10). Teaching Children Life Skills. Thrive.

Thriveadmin. (2022). Protecting Our Kids: Teaching Children About Personal Safety. *Bravehearts*.

Worzbyt, J. C. (2004). *Teaching Kids to Care and to be Careful: A Practical Guide for Teachers, Counselors, and Parents*. R&L Education.

Wright, L. W. (2023). Personal Safety and Stranger Danger: How to Teach Your Child. *Understood*.

Made in the USA
Columbia, SC
28 September 2023